The Women of Quyi

Why has the female voice—as the resonant incarnation of the female body—inspired both fascination and ambivalence? Why were women restricted from performing on the Chinese public stage? How have female roles and voices been appropriated by men throughout much of the history of Chinese theatre? Why were the women of *quyi*—a community of Chinese female singers in Republican Tianjin—able to become successful, respected artists when other female singers and actors in competing performance traditions struggled for acceptance? Drawing substantially on original ethnographic fieldwork conducted in the 1980s and 1990s, Francesca R. Sborgi Lawson offers answers to these questions and demonstrates how the women of *quyi* successfully negotiated their sexuality and vocality in performance. Owing to their role as third-person narrators, the women of *quyi* bridged the gender gap, creating an androgynous persona that de-emphasized their feminine appearance and, at the same time, allowed them to showcase their female voices on public stages—places that had been previously unwelcoming to female artists. This is a story about female storytellers who sang their way to respectability and social change in the early decades of the twentieth century by minimizing their bodies in order to allow their voices to be heard.

Francesca R. Sborgi Lawson received an undergraduate degree in harp performance from Brigham Young University, USA, a Master's degree in ethnomusicology from University of California, Los Angeles, and a Ph.D. in ethnomusicology from the University of Washington. She conducted research on the inter-relationships of language and music in the narrative arts of Tianjin, China as a Fulbright-Hays and National Academy of Sciences Research Fellow. She also worked as a President's Postdoctoral Research Fellow at the University of Illinois at Urbana-Champaign and at the University of California at Berkeley and taught courses in the Asian humanities and in gender-music relationships at Columbia University in New York City. She is currently the Humanities Professor of Ethnomusicology in the Department of Comparative Arts and Letters at Brigham Young University and the 2015 winner of the Jaap Kunst prize for the most significant article published in the field of ethnomusicology. Her first book, *The Narrative Arts of Tianjin: Between Music and Language*, was published by Ashgate in 2011 as part of the SOAS ethnomusicology series.

SOAS Musicology Series
Series Editor:
Keith Howard, SOAS, *University of London, UK*

The study of the world's many and diverse music cultures has become an important part of the discipline of musicology. Often termed 'ethnomusicology', the resulting studies share the fundamental recognition that music is cherished by every society in the world. Like language, music is a universal means of individual and cultural expression. It is also infinitely varied. Music in any society has intrinsic value in its own right, and can tell us much about the culture in which it developed. The core of the SOAS Musicology Series comprises studies of different musics, analysed in the contexts of the societies of which they are part, and exploring repertories, performance practice, musical instruments, and the roles and impacts of individual composers and performers. Studies which integrate music with dance, theatre or the visual arts are encouraged, and contextualised studies of music within the Western art canon are not excluded.

Reflecting current ethnomusicological theory and practice, the editors recognize the value of interdisciplinary and collaborative research. Volumes may utilize methodologies developed in anthropology, sociology, linguistics and psychology to explore music; they may seek to create a dialogue between scholars and musicians; or they may primarily be concerned with the evaluation of historical documentation. Monographs that explore contemporary and popular musics, the effect of globalization on musical production, or the comparison of different music cultures are also welcomed.

Recent titles in the series:

The Women of Quyi

Liminal Voices and Androgynous Bodies

Francesca R. Sborgi Lawson

Routledge
Taylor & Francis Group

LONDON AND NEW YORK

First published 2017
by Routledge
2 Park Square, Milton Park, Abingdon, Oxon OX14 4RN

and by Routledge
711 Third Avenue, New York, NY 10017

Routledge is an imprint of the Taylor & Francis Group, an informa
business

British Library Cataloguing-in-Publication Data
A catalogue record for this book is available from the British Library

Library of Congress Cataloging-in-Publication Data
A catalog record for this book has been requested

ISBN: 978-1-138-23413-0 (hbk)
ISBN: 978-1-315-30787-9 (ebk)

Typeset in Times New Roman by
Servis Filmsetting Ltd, Stockport, Cheshire

Contents

List of Figures

List of Music Examples

Acknowledgments

I would like to thank many people for their substantial assistance in supporting my work on this book. Particular thanks go to the Humanities Center at BYU for a generous grant to workshop the manuscript. In particular, I would like to thank Margaret Wan from the University of Utah, Brandie Siegfried, my colleague at Brigham Young University, and Matt Wickman, my colleague and the Director of the Humanities Center at BYU, for their careful reading of this work. Their comments and suggestions have been invaluable. The Department of Comparative Arts and Letters, the community of scholars in Women's Studies, and the College of Humanities at Brigham Young University also provided support and encouragement during the writing and editing process, which I humbly and gratefully acknowledge.

Nate Thatcher painstakingly transferred all my musical transcriptions to a digital format, and Lin Guo digitized the Chinese texts in Appendices 1–3; I thank them both for their skills. Michael Needham provided invaluable assistance in reviewing this manuscript, and I am sincerely grateful to him and his staff at Humanities First for their meticulous work.

The editorial staff at Routledge has been generous and especially helpful in preparing this manuscript for publication. In particular, I wish to thank the two anonymous reviewers for their astute observations and suggestions that have dramatically improved this manuscript. I am especially grateful to Emma Gallon and her editorial staff for their expertise, professionalism, and goodwill as they have guided me throughout the process of publication.

Finally, I wish to recognize Professor Xue Baokun, my former mentor at Nankai University, my two teachers, Ms. Wang Yubao and Ms. Lu Yiqin, and my selfless research assistant, Ms. Bao Zhenpei. These individuals have been committed to assisting me with my research since the first day I met them, and I am deeply grateful for their help and friendship over the past several decades. Most importantly, I want to recognize all the women of *quyi* whose stories have been the inspiration for this work; I humbly dedicate this book to them. My husband, John Lawson, ultimately helped everything to come together, and to him I owe the greatest thanks.

Note on the Text

Chinese vocabulary used in this book is Romanized according to the *pinyin* system without tone marks. A glossary of selected Chinese characters corresponding to an alphabetized list of the Romanized words is found in Appendix 6.

When heard outside of the context of the Tianjin narrative arts community, the "r" at the end of words such as "far" and "qiar" is pronounced as an "n" in standard Mandarin. However, throughout this book I have Romanized these words according to the way they are pronounced in the narrative arts communities throughout north China and not according to standard Mandarin spelling.

My musical transcription of the vocal schools discussed in Chapter 3 is found in Appendix 4, and my musical transcription of "Listening" is found in Appendix 5. The Chinese texts for the poems I translate in Chapter 2 are found in Appendices 1 and 3, respectively. Additionally, the complete text for the Comic Monologue I summarize in Chapter 2 is found in Appendix 2.

Prologue

Arrival

I had not planned to research female vocalists when I first arrived at Nankai University in Tianjin on a dry September afternoon in 1985.[1] Instead, I was mentally prepared to study the relationships of music and language in the narrative genres known as *quyi*,[2] for which the city was nationally famous. Anxious to get started, I began attending performances by members of the Tianjin Municipal *Quyi* Arts Troupe and requesting interviews with those performers. My discovery of the central position of powerful female singers in the troupe came during my first interview.

When I first approached the study of language–music relationships in *quyi*, I had hoped to interview some of the older performers who had been influential in shaping the workings of the community over the past several decades. I was told that the then 69-year-old Master Li[3] was one of the most famous performers in Tianjin, but that I would probably not be granted an interview with her—she was virtually inaccessible. Much to my surprise, however, several weeks after my first inquiry, I received a phone call that she would be coming to see me that afternoon.

Hurriedly, I contacted one of the faculty members who was asked to work with me at Nankai University, my official sponsoring organization, or *danwei*—a required connection for every foreign resident. He was also caught off guard by this sudden visit and was worried about preparing adequately for the event, so he abruptly changed his plans for the day to accommodate her visit. I was surprised by the anxious reaction of this otherwise reserved and self-contained man. He was a distinguished researcher at the leading university in Tianjin and a nationally recognized scholar in his own right.

Shortly after the appointed time, a limousine drove up to the entrance of the foreign guesthouse at Nankai, where I was living. The appearance of a limousine was highly unusual, even in Tianjin; aside from this occasion, I never saw anyone else arrive or leave by limousine before or during my stay in China. As the driver came around to escort Master Li to meet the entourage that had assembled in front of the guesthouse, I noticed that Master Li commanded everyone's respect as a *da renwu*, a VIP. All in attendance bowed and paid obeisance to her.

After she settled into her chair in the conference room, I began asking the questions that I had already mailed to her (and to all the other people whom I had hoped to interview) shortly after my arrival in China. The professor, my assistant, and I were dismayed to see that she refused to answer any of my questions. Whenever I brought up an issue, she circumvented it. My assistant used the term *baoliu* ("withhold") to describe the manner in which Master Li responded to my questions. At the time, I could not understand why she had agreed to come.

Selecting a teacher

When I later expressed my concern about the failed interview attempt, one of the Nankai officials suggested that I might have more success speaking to Master Li's *tudi* (disciple),[4] a middle-aged woman named Master Hua who was highly intelligent and articulate. There were two possible reasons that my contacts at Nankai had suggested that I contact Hua rather than Li. It may have been that they were concerned that I would not be able to pursue a relationship with Master Li under any circumstance, so Master Hua would be my best bet to gain entrance into the community. It may also have been that they preferred Master Hua over Master Li simply because of Master Hua's congeniality—Confucian etiquette notwithstanding. No matter the reason, an interview with Master Hua was much easier to arrange. Master Hua was so genuinely helpful that, at the suggestion of two of my Nankai colleagues, I decided to ask her if I could become her disciple—or the disciple of Master Li's disciple, thus establishing a formal relationship with Master Hua in the eyes of the entire community. Becoming a disciple meant that I would, in essence, belong to Hua and to her artistic tradition. By virtue of that relationship, people in the community would more easily accept and know how to respond to me. This was important in mitigating my obvious other identity as a foreigner, as I would have both a connection to a respected tradition and an identity as a surrogate member of the group.

The only problem with my request was that I would be sidestepping the authority of Master Li by not selecting her, thereby bypassing the proper channels of authority.[5] Since many of my contacts at Nankai University downplayed the issue, however, I believed that Hua would be preferable as the teacher and facilitator of my research. I had no guarantee that Li would be any more willing to help me if I were her disciple than she had been at our first meeting, whereas Hua had been approachable from the outset.

Several months went by before I received any news from the Tianjin Municipal *Quyi* Arts Troupe. Li was angrier than anyone had anticipated, and she was not going to allow her disciple to be the first Tianjinese to have a foreign disciple without resistance.[6] In retrospect, I believe that Master Li may have withheld information at our initial meeting because she was waiting for me to initiate a proper relationship with her—my inexperience had led to ignorance of cultural etiquette. While I waited for word from the troupe about Hua, I was able to study unofficially with another performer from the troupe, Master Liu, because she was free of any relational entanglements. Finally, Li gave in to pressure from Nankai University and consented, and I was given permission to hold a ceremony in which I would become the disciple of both Masters Hua and Liu.[7] Li ultimately gave in to my request to establish this tie with Hua, but her stalling was a deliberate move to curtail my research and to punish me for not selecting her as a teacher.[8]

The ceremony (*Baishihui*)

During the *baishihui*, an official ceremony in which a disciple is granted the opportunity to begin studying with a master performer, Li delivered a speech that reflected her displeasure toward me in a way that was calculated to make me lose face in front of all those present.[9] While on the most superficial level her speech both extolled my decision to honor the older members of the community and chided some of the other younger performers of the troupe for not following my "filial" example, it was also a rather trenchant criticism of me for favoring the disciple over the master—a point that will be discussed in greater detail in Chapter 4.

I spent the following month in intensive study of narrative performance with Hua. I met with Hua on an almost daily basis, and in the process learned much about both the genre and the discipleship process. After the ceremony she told me that, as her disciple, I was now considered part of her family and that she would provide all the help I needed for my research. This particular relationship allowed me entrance into the community that would have been otherwise impossible. She later explained:

> Why should we have a *baishihui*? We have this because we need to have a procedure—a legal procedure. After going through the ceremony, both sides have officially agreed to the relationship. It is a way of leaving a record behind for all to see—an announcement to the entire community. The idea is that the master has a responsibility towards the disciple's progress, and the disciple agrees to wholeheartedly study everything the master teaches. A serious performer *must* have a master; otherwise, she is considered an amateur.
>
> (Hua 1991)

By sealing my relationship to my teachers in this very public ceremony, I was demonstrating to the community that I was sufficiently filial, deferent, and serious about learning the traditions. I created a subordinate identity in the field by initiating this connection,[10] and I hasten to add, I never deluded myself into thinking that I was on a par with a native-born female performer.

Part of a community

After creating an identity in the community through a social relationship with two respected teachers, I quickly realized the vital importance of strict loyalty to the group;[11] I saw that a relationship with a teacher allowed me to enter into a privileged, culturally charged liminal space. Yang's comment about creating boundaries between oneself and others is instructive:

> Rather than creating discrete and unified ontological categories of persons ... it appears that the Chinese subscribe to a relational construction of persons ... Chinese personhood and personal identity are not given in the abstract as something intrinsic to and fixed in human nature, but are constantly being created, altered, and dismantled in particular social relationships. As a result, Chinese culture presents a frequent lack of clear-cut boundaries between self and other.
>
> (1989: 39)

Establishing a relationship between a teacher and a disciple implies a process that evolves during the course of their careers—a process explored in more detail in Chapter 4. Even though the possibility of movement within this social space is both real and expected, the idea of forging a relationship with a competitor from a different school of singing would have been the equivalent of blasphemy. In other words, although I was creating new relationships that would shift and change over time, those relationships were delimited and circumscribed by my responsibilities and loyalties towards my teachers. Although it would have been enlightening to work with Li as well, the nature of my relationship with Hua precluded any further contact with Li because of the professional rivalry between them.[12] In fact, there would have been no way that one researcher could have interviewed both women and gotten reliable information from either of them, since an outsider may establish allegiance to only one of two conflicting parties. If researchers were foolish enough to jeopardize their standing in the community by cultivating relationships with people who are perceived as outsiders, they would not only anger members of their group, but they would also lose the respect of the group's rivals, who would also decry the disloyalty.[13] Hence, developing professional relationships is only possible with individuals between whom there is an established connection—like the one established in the *baishihui*—or with people who are part of one's existing relational web of contacts.

In the process of discovering the importance of becoming part of the community, I had to confront the fact that my chosen associations would automatically preclude contacts with their rivals. One of the consequences of situating myself in the field was acknowledging that my research would be partial, not only by virtue of my role as a foreign ethnographer but also because of my status as a member of a particular artistic tradition within the community. If another researcher had established relationships with a rival group, he or she would have experienced the same general restrictions and privileges and would have produced a study quite different from my own.

The need to stay within one's circle of consultants was reinforced when I tried to contact another American researcher who was studying another performer of the same *quyi* genre. Master Hua severely reprimanded me for going outside our circle of established relationships, and warned me that any other infraction would nullify her obligation to teach me.

Becoming a musical disciple also means experiencing firsthand the web of social entanglements inherent in musical relationships. This study is based on interviews with members of an exclusive community to whom I had professional access and on literary and musical analyses of some of the great masterworks of Tianjin *quyi*. As such, this book is a celebration of the idiosyncratic, as it comments on a particular constellation of historical circumstances that allowed a select group of women to use their voices in public performance as a means for social mobility, creating a feminine discourse that was important both for the overt semantic message of the texts and for the way in which the messages were communicated through a uniquely female voice.

Notes

1 While I did the most of my initial research during my first field trip to Tianjin from 1985 to 1986, and briefly again in 1987, much of the information contained in the following chapters was obtained from a series of interviews I conducted from December 1990 through January 1991.

2 *Quyi* may be roughly translated as "the narrative arts." Originally these genres were called *shuochang* ("speaking-singing"), but the name was later changed to *quyi* (Lawson 2011: 23). For an introduction to a selected number of these genres in the city of Tianjin, see Lawson 2011: 7–23.

3 With the exception of performers with well-documented careers such as Liu Baoquan (1869–1942), Zhang Cuifeng (1913–1975), Luo Yusheng (1914–2002), Sun Shujun (1922–2011), Xiao Lanyun (1923–1992), Shi Huiru (1923–1967), Wang Yubao (1926–), and Lu Yiqin (1933–), I have changed the names of all my other consultants and refer to them only by their fictitious surnames. I have also altered many of the superficial details regarding my encounters with them because of the sensitive nature of the information they shared with me.

4 I use the word disciple to translate *tudi*, a word that connotes a highly formalized relationship with her master teacher. See Chapter 4 for a discussion about why master teachers need to acquire disciples.

5 According to Confucian etiquette, no one should favor a younger person over her older, more experienced teacher. This is true regardless of Li's apparent unwillingness to answer my questions (Lawson 2011: 36–37).

6 A precedent for foreigners studying *quyi* had already been established by Catherine Stevens, who studied with Zhang Cuifeng in Taiwan in the 1960s and with Sun Shujun in Beijing in the 1980s and 1990s. See Stevens 1975, 1990, 2011.

7 In addition to these two teachers, I also studied informally with several other performers, including some male performers of spoken genres.

8 Withholding one's favor is a common strategy used to curtail another's success. See chapter 4 for more examples of this strategy.

9 For more information about "face" in the context of the *quyi* community, see Lawson (2011: 35).

10 See Yang (1989: 39) for more information about the importance of forming relationships in Chinese society.

11 The issue of establishing connections is also discussed in more detail in Lawson (2011: 31–46).

12 Apparently the rivalry had existed before my arrival, but my presence in the community and my selection of Hua as my teacher exacerbated the contention. Chapter 4 includes a more detailed discussion of rivalries between masters and disciples.

13 While my decision to select two teachers may appear to contradict this point, I was careful to select two women who were not competitors; rather, they were congenial associates representing completely different genres. Those perceived as outsiders are either rival counterparts from the same genre or other performers from outside the Troupe.

Introduction

The triumph of the voice

I begin with two fictitious stories, each based on a composite of biographical narratives gleaned from my interviews with female narrators about prostitute singers[1] in the early decades of the twentieth century—singers whose lives seemed to have been impelled by the outcomes of the tragic heroines they portrayed through song. The following accounts confirm Gail Hershatter's conjecture that many women were tricked into prostitution (1986: 208) and demonstrate the advantages of singing for talented women whose superior vocal skills eventually enabled them to leave prostitution.

A piece of silver[2]

Tan was eight years old when her father sold her to a brothel in order to support his opium habit. At the time, she did not understand what her father was trying to do. When she and her father entered the brothel, the owner was interested in seeing if she had any illnesses or handicaps, so he asked her to perform. Innocently, she did a somersault and the owner gave her father a piece of silver. This was the last time Tan ever saw her father.

Children at the brothel were usually not allowed to entertain clients until they reached fourteen, so Tan and three other young girls took care of all the housekeeping chores. When Tan turned fourteen, the couple that owned the brothel decided that she might be a good candidate for studying vocal storytelling (*quyi*) because she was beautiful and had an elegant demeanor. They reasoned that if Tan were good, she would bring prestige to the brothel and would attract higher-class and higher-paying customers, so they sent her to a good teacher in hopes of training her as a performer who would raise the cultural and economic status of the brothel. Tan's freedom from a life of prostitution enabled her to concentrate all of her energy on her musical skills and kept her free from social stigmas.

While Tan escaped having to give sexual favors to clients, she was not spared the beatings and torture that were a routine part of life in the brothel. Girls were often beaten simply to remind them that they were slaves. The face was the only part of their bodies that was spared, since all the women work-ing there had to appear attractive to patrons.

If a beating with a whip did not keep the girls in line, the brothel owners employed more sinister methods. Tan recalls that one of the worst experi-ences she witnessed was the punishment of a friend who tried to resist a client. The owners stripped her from the waist down and tied a bag around her in which they had placed a starving cat. As they whipped the bag, the cat clawed the girl, ripping her skin. The owners then shut the girl in a room and deprived her of food and water for three days. This type of abuse was designed to frighten Tan and the other girls into submission, but by no means was the most extreme; some of the owners' other forms of torture were so traumatic that Tan could not bear to recount them.

When Tan turned sixteen, she was ready to make her debut. To ensure applause for her first performance, the owners arranged for a vociferous claque. She was given new clothes, jewelry, a carriage, and two attendants every time she had to travel, but she was constantly reminded that nothing belonged to her. Like all the other girls, she could not come and go as she pleased, as she was under constant surveillance by the attendants.

One night the madam of the brothel came to her room after a perfor-mance and rifled through her belongings without saying a word. Afterwards the madam beat Tan ruthlessly. "All your things are still the same things we gave you. There is nothing new here. Why haven't the patrons been giving you gifts? You must earn gifts from the clients!" For the first time, Tan understood that despite her training in *quyi*, she was simply a prostitute with a different set of skills.

Tan began to notice that one of the patrons who came regularly to hear her was the twenty-seven-year-old son of an army officer in the Guomindang.[3] When he made it known that he was interested in Tan, the brothel owners became concerned that this officer's son would take her away from the brothel without paying. Tan had always hoped that a man would eventually buy her so that she would escape living in the brothel, and, sensing that they might lose their investment, the owners incarcerated Tan in her room. Tan wanted to drown herself, but the owner, keenly aware of the possibility of suicide, kept close tabs on her.

Heartbroken, the son of the army officer tried to poison himself. As the oldest son, he was heir to his father's fortune and the key link in the patriarchal line, so, in order to prevent further tragedy, the family relented to his wishes and arranged to procure Tan. Since the brothel owners realized this influential military family had the power to close their brothel at any time, they released Tan from her incarceration and sent her to the family with the stipulation that she had to give back all the clothing and jewelry she had acquired as a performer. She was allowed to keep only one belt and the clothes on her back.

Tan's life in the home of the military official was not an improvement. The family emphasized that she, as a singer from a brothel, could never aspire to becoming the wife of the eldest son in an aristocratic home—an honor with privileges beyond her station—so there was no ceremony recognizing their relationship. In essence, she was again living the life of a prostitute. The son slept in a large room of his own, and she slept in the servant's quarters. Her life was made miserable by incessant insults and derision; the family mocked her by saying, "Aren't you the one that sings? Like painted-face performers in opera?" When Tan tried to serve tea, they would often throw the tray back at her, breaking all the dishes.

Tan gave birth to a daughter, but the parents did not take notice, and the fact that the baby was a girl only exacerbated the situation. The family nurse, however, took pity on Tan and showed her how to care for the baby. Six years after she entered the household, the Chinese Communist Party overthrew the Guomindang. Both the father and his son were imprisoned, and the father was eventually executed. The son remained in prison for fifteen years, and Tan maintained no contact with him.

Even though Tan had not performed while she lived with the family, she had not forgotten her musical skills. As an outstanding performer, Tan was recognized and supported by the new government in 1949, and was able to support her child with dignity. For the first time in her life, she felt as though she was living a human existence. She later became one of the outstanding members of the Tianjin Municipal *Quyi* Arts Troupe, and her daughter eventually graduated from college—an outcome that would have been impossible had Tan been forced into a life of prostitution.

For her family

Unlike Tan, Du was raised by her natal family. As members of the desperately poor underclass in Tianjin, Du's parents worked at unstable professions for substandard wages. The men in the family performed heavy labor and the mother worked as a prostitute. While the mother's job was considered more degrading than her husband's, she was able to earn more in a couple of days than her husband could earn in a month. They were able to save a little money for Du to study *quyi* in order for her to help support the family.

Financial difficulties persisted, however. When Du's older brother was ready to be married, the family was unable to provide the necessary brideprice. Marriage of the oldest son was a cultural necessity for both rich and poor, since the survival of the parents depended on living with the oldest son, so while the father was on a trip to the countryside to see his mother's family, his mother suggested that they sell Du, who was twelve years old, into prostitution. Her first client, a thirty-year-old man who had been coming to the brothel to hear her sing *quyi*, told her that her mother had instructed him to take her after the performance. Because Du recognized the man, she did not hesitate to go with him; however, she became increasingly uneasy when he took her to a hotel and told her that her mother would come for her. Finally, the man admitted that her mother had arranged for her to spend the night with him to pay for her brother's engagement and wedding expenses.

That first experience marked Du as an adult who could provide sexual services. She worked first as a performer and entertained clients afterwards in order to help support her family. When her mother died a few years later, Du's salary paid for the funeral. Though desperately unhappy, Du saved enough money to put her younger brother and sister through school to help them to escape the hardships of the underclass.

Eventually, a wealthy businessman whose first wife could not conceive offered to buy Du if she would bear his son. He ended up paying her a good deal of money, which she sent back to her natal family. The man considered her no more than a plaything, however, and she was treated poorly in the home. When she gave birth to a daughter, the man no longer wanted her, telling her that the arrangement was for her to provide a son. He gave her a lump sum and dismissed her and her baby. Fortunately, his payment was sufficient for her to survive until she was able to work as a female narrator after the end of the Chinese civil war.

After 1949, most female performers who had also worked as prostitutes were not able to continue performing *quyi*. In most cases, prostitutes had not received proper musical training, and the women who emerged as respected performers had to be superior musicians. While a young female performer might have previously been able to get by on appearance, she would not have been able to survive as a performer for finicky connoisseurs in Tianjin. Because Du was exceptionally talented, had studied with skilled teachers, and had an excellent reputation in the community, she was one of the few prostitutes who gained entrance into the Tianjin Municipal *Quyi* Arts Troupe when it was founded in 1952. Most of Du's colleagues knew about her background, but she was never shunned or ostracized. Less talented performers with less checkered pasts did not survive as performers in the post-1949 society, but Du went on to have a distinguished career, raise her daughter by herself, and live to see her grandchildren flourish.

While most of the other lowborn women who performed *quyi* came from more fortunate circumstances than Tan and Du, the key to their success was the same as for singers who emerged from brothels: the ability to downplay sexuality and emphasize their voices, achieving an optimal balance between voice and body. Tan and Du's real-life scenarios are reminiscent of the intolerable injustices faced by heroines like Decima in "The Courtesan's Jewel Box"[4]—except the real-life women were eventually able to become socially mobile because of their training in *quyi*, particularly as they sang stories about maltreated women. Indeed, the act of telling well-known stories about wronged heroines endowed female storytellers with power to overcome their lowborn status, enabling them to sue for redress through their plaintive renditions.

Although only a small number of female narrators began their careers as prostitute singers, the stories of Tan and Du exemplify the triumph of the voice for approximately two dozen female narrators in the city of Tianjin, the third-largest city in China, during the early to middle decades of the twentieth century. This book is an exploration into the heroines about whom they sang and the curious relationships that evolved between the singers and the protagonists of their stories. Few biographies of female narrators from the city of Tianjin are in print,[5] and my fieldwork alerted me to a community that I would never have discovered had I relied solely on archival research. I came to know the women of *quyi* in the mid-1980s and early 1990s, when many of them had already retired. Since then, several of these women have become extremely frail or have passed away, and this work is designed as a tribute to all the women of *quyi*.

Inspired by the recent groundbreaking narrative *Bright Star of the West* about the late Irish *sean-nós* singer Joe Heaney, this study was initially instigated by fieldwork and later illuminated through analysis and contemplation of a bygone era from the early twentieth century. The decades since my first field trip have helped me grasp the historical significance of these female performers, as I have considered the wealth of recent research in Chinese opera, gender studies, and musicology,[6] allowing for a more interdisciplinary engagement of issues than would have been possible at the time of my original field project. The passage of time has also allowed me to contemplate how best to communicate some of the sensitive information I first acquired as a young researcher. *explanation of the delay*

Quyi

Appreciating the significance of female narrators in the cultural history of twentieth-century Tianjin requires a basic understanding of *quyi*, which is the modern name for the pan-Chinese narrative traditions that have charmed and entertained Chinese audiences for centuries.[7] While over 150 varieties of storytelling have been documented throughout China (Zhang 1983: 11–14), certain areas of the country have favored the development of the narrative arts over others due to demographics. The special popularity of *quyi* in Tianjin was a direct response to the city's rise as a major industrial and commercial center in northern China in the early twentieth century. The development of foreign trade and the emergence of new industries lured thousands of workers from the famine-stricken countryside in order to seek their fortunes (Hershatter 1986: 40–41), and teahouses, brothels, and small theaters proliferated throughout Tianjin to accommodate the ever-increasing numbers of urban workers hungry for entertainment after work (Xue 1985a). Even though *quyi* also thrived in the nearby capital of Beijing, the greater number of industrial workers in Tianjin provided more performance opportunities for *quyi* artists, giving rise to the epithet "*Quyi* was born in Beijing, but blossomed in Tianjin" (*quyi zai Beijing sheng, Tianjin zhang*). Two important counterparts to the narrative arts in Tianjin are *pingtan* from the Shanghai-Suzhou area and *nanyin* from Guangzhou, but scores of other variants exist throughout the country (Zhang 1983: 11–13). In each Chinese narrative form, the interplay between the local dialect and indigenous popular melodies creates a synergy between music and language that entertains through the narrative and delights through musical beauty.

The spectacular development of the narrative arts in Tianjin was also a result of the association between educated amateur authors and unlettered professional performers as they worked together to accommodate the needs of their urban clientele. Peasant storytellers, who had migrated to the city and brought with them the tales they had performed for other peasants during the winter, now found themselves obliged to shorten their repertoires in order to cater to the schedules of the urban working classes (Stevens 1975: 81). Prostitutes and itinerant beggars joined the motley group of performers, all of whom benefitted from their association with skilled amateur writers who composed lyrics for their newly adapted stories (Xue 1985a). The unique collaboration between authors and performers resulted in an especially congenial union that benefitted performer and patron alike. The literariness of the texts appealed particularly to the educated members of the audiences, and the dazzling vocal skills of the singers and storytellers were attractive to all who came to witness these performances, winning for *quyi* the epithet *yasugongshang*, which means "appealing to both refined and popular tastes." For performers, *quyi* was a creative outlet for which there was an eager clientele, providing a steady income when their skills were good. For patrons, *quyi* was primarily a source of inexpensive and ubiquitous entertainment. Urban workers briefly forgot the tedium and hardship of their lives when they indulged in an afternoon or evening of *quyi* in a teahouse theater.

Given the existing distinction between the plaintively sung genres and the slapstick spoken forms, female performers discovered a natural performance opportunity in the vocal genres, particularly since many of the sung stories popular in the narrative arts community were about virtuous women (Stevens 1975: 89–90; Xue 1985a). Moreover, at a time in Chinese history when the modernizing nation was becoming increasingly aware of women's rights as an international issue, many female performers in Tianjin confidently took to the public stage and sang about heroines in a highly ornate vocal style—a style that was noticeably different from that of their male colleagues (Xue 1985a). These female performers eventually drove away their male competitors in the sung genres, and male performers began to specialize in the spoken genres, reflecting the popular saying *nanshuo nüchang* (men speak, women sing).

The distinction between the feminine sung genres and the masculine spoken genres was still in effect when I first came to Tianjin in 1985—some six decades after the widespread appearance of female narrators on urban stages. As I learned about female narrators who began their careers in the early decades of the Chinese Republic (1912–1949), I was astonished by their story. Since the fall of the Mongols in the fourteenth century, Confucianism dictated that women of good breeding must not sing or act on public stages, and that prohibition was forcefully renewed by the Emperor Qianlong's 1722 ban on female public performance (Harris and Pease 2013: 2). While there is plenty of evidence of Chinese female vocality in folk song, narrative song, courtesan traditions, and private theatrical performances, I had never before heard about Chinese women who had achieved undisputed artistic success by using their singing voices to wrest a public performance tradition from male competitors, nor had I ever read about or witnessed the kind of social machinations I saw in a society composed primarily of women. The women of *quyi* in Tianjin were extraordinary, and their exceptionalism was due, in large part, to the way they claimed their feminine singing voices by de-emphasizing their bodies. In this book I distinguish between two parts of the body: the audible yet invisible "grain" of the voice (see Barthes 1977: 181–183) and the visible body that produces it. My claim is that by emphasizing the invisible sound and minimizing the visible body, the women of *quyi* were in a position to be *heard* as artists rather than *seen* as sexual beings. Further, the androgynous women of *quyi* achieved their success by engaging in quintessentially Chinese cultural practices and strategies. In many ways, these women epitomized what I find to be most fascinating about the Chinese—their ability to explore cultural areas I call *liminal spaces*.

Liminality and the women of *Quyi*

Based roughly on Richard Schechner's conception of liminality,[8] which is "inherently 'in between' and therefore cannot be pinned down or located exactly" (1998: 360), liminal spaces are the rich areas between two cultural extremes, and many Chinese art forms explore a fundamental, inherent complementarity between contrastive cultural elements that are constantly re-creating one another. The examples of liminal space investigated in this work include the areas between lived reality and imagination; linguistic word-tone and melody in performance; conventional male and female genders in literary depiction and on stage; and the constantly changing roles between masters and their pupils in the realm of social interaction. Driven by an urge to seek complementarity between opposing forces, the Chinese embrace liminal areas between those forces as loci of artistic discovery and social negotiation, and the women of *quyi* successfully mastered the ability to find "sweet spots" in key liminal spaces as they navigated their roles as third-person storytellers in Republican Chinese culture (from approximately 1911–1949). As Ellen Koskoff reminds us, "women who are outside both male and female norms (i.e., shamans, prostitutes, midwives, lesbians, witches, and so on) are often awarded certain musical freedoms not given to women who adhere to their prescribed roles" (2014: 26). The women of *quyi* aptly fit this description. Moreover, according to the people I interviewed in the 1980s and early 1990s, the distinctive successes achieved by female narrators were based on their ability to mine their circumstances according to the unique configuration of historical and cultural forces that characterized the Republican period in early twentieth-century China. Their greatest success was in appropriating feminine portrayals from male competitors in the narrative arts and from female impersonators in opera who had heretofore monopolized the depiction of femininity on public stages.

Implicit in the notion of co-opting female roles and voices is the question of why it was even necessary in the first place. Why had male singers appropriated female voices? Moreover, why did women have to de-emphasize their bodies in order to be heard as singers? As Dunn and Jones claim, "the voices of women ... have inspired the greatest fascination, as well as the deepest ambivalence" (2001: i), and the women of *quyi* were unusually successful because they capitalized on the fascination and minimized the ambivalence through their skills as androgynous performers, using liminality to their advantage.

Contents

Chapter 1 discusses the ubiquitous "female voice and body problem" that has plagued female performers throughout history. I provide selected examples of the voice and body problem in Western European and Chinese musical theater to demonstrate the enormous amounts of energy that were spent to contain female performers, or to completely remove them from public stages. One of the most fascinating solutions to the voice and body problem in China has been for female impersonators known as male *dan* to perform female roles and sing in a falsetto voice, creating a simulacrum of feminine reality to supplant actual female performers—a representation I call the *metaphysical feminine*.[9] In using the word "metaphysical," I am not invoking the antagonistic dualisms inherent in the Derridean notion of metaphysics; rather, I am recuperating the meaning of the word to refer to supernatural characters—beloved literary and theatrical figures who possess both male and female features. In Chinese performance, the male *dan* were able to assume the roles of metaphysical feminine characters because of their androgyny; similarly, the women of *quyi* were in a position to sing stories about metaphysical feminine characters due to their roles as androgynous storytellers.[10] However, unlike the male *dan*, whose androgynous portrayals were eventually seen to be at odds with the politics of nation building in the later years of the Republic, the empowered women of *quyi* exemplified the progressive ideals of the Chinese Republic and were therefore able to take full advantage of their position as modern women, all the while benefitting from the metaphysical feminine archetypes that symbolically endowed them with cherished cultural values. The women of *quyi* appropriated metaphysical femininity, de-emphasized their bodies in performance, and maximized their vocal talents to avoid a place I refer to as the "danger zone"—a performance space where the voice and body problem is most acute—where female performers are eroticized rather than acknowledged and respected as artists. Their success in creating an androgynous image on stage while still preserving the feminine singing voice alleviated many of the issues associated with the voice and body problem that beset so many other female performers.

Chapter 2 explores the stories about metaphysical heroines sung by the women of *quyi*, beginning with a translation and commentary on the extraordinary tale about a young female vocal prodigy named Bai Niu, whose vocal talents were romanticized in the novel *Laocan Youji*. Her story became an allegory for the women of *quyi*, who appropriated similar stories about other androgynous female characters as they performed on public stages in Republican Tianjin. After an explanation of their literary and theatrical origins, four other texts featuring metaphysical heroines are highlighted in this chapter, exemplifying the attributes of tactical intelligence, virtuous self-sacrifice, and tragic ill treatment. The last text, *Listening to the Bells at Sword Pavilion*, is translated in its entirety and given special importance as one of the great masterworks in narrative literature. This poem about a grieving emperor features his deceased wife as an absent heroine, offering an invitation for a female narrator to become her auditory presence. Once women were given the opportunity to sing such texts, female narrators used their own corporeal voices to conjure up the metaphysical heroines of their stories. In doing so, the women of *quyi* became the musical successors to the male authors and performers who first created metaphysical femininity.

Building on the discussions about metaphysical feminine texts, Chapter 3 discusses how Chinese female singers were able to fulfill the meaning of their metaphysical feminine texts through their vocal artistry, simultaneously pushing the boundaries of semantic meaning, unleashing musical beauty, and creating an exchange between the arts of music and literature in liminal space. When female narrators first captivated their audiences with their distinctly feminine voices, they created a vocal sensation comparable to the literary impression made by Bai Niu. As female singers gradually monopolized the performance of sung genres in the narrative arts, singing became viewed as a quintessentially feminine form of expression. In order to demonstrate the way these genres were feminized, the first half of this chapter compares two musical renditions of a story, providing an analysis of the stylistic differences that make one male and the other female in the Beijing Drumsong tradition, which is one of the most revered genres in Tianjin *quyi*. The female school founded by Luo Yusheng is significant because she consciously created a lyrical melodic style that suited the stories about metaphysical heroines. Luo is viewed as an innovator, having won first prize for her golden recording of *Listening to the Bells at Sword Pavilion* in 1989. The second half of the chapter analyzes her brilliant musical lyricism in setting this text, which became her signature work.

With the growing popularity of women as narrative singers, master performers needed female disciples to whom they could pass on their tradition. Chapter 4 highlights the ways in which women navigated social space as teachers and disciples within the matriarchal society that emerged in the Tianjin *quyi* community from the middle to late decades of the twentieth century. The master–disciple relationships I studied were both fluid and highly antagonistic, and disciples became proficient at employing a repertoire of social behaviors in order to eventually challenge and manipulate their status. Performers tacitly recognized that a disciple's subordinate position implied both an important hidden power vis-à-vis the master teacher and a base from which to negotiate that power and potentially subvert the hierarchy. The power of the subordinate position of the disciple is significant because it demonstrates how low-born female performers are empowered to challenge boundaries by utilizing the two major tactics involved in the cultural strategy known as *guanxi*: currying favor to improve one's status and withholding favor to curtail another's status. Assuming either a superior or subordinate role involved both tactics at key points in master–disciple relationships. Three case studies are given to illustrate patterns evident in the interaction of superior–subordinate role types in the popular *quyi* genre known as Comic Routines. The examples of women who successfully utilized the adaptive strategies implied by the roles of the actors in Comic Routines demonstrate the importance of observing a variety of female experiences and of looking to performance as a means for shedding light on the complex relationships among women in China.

The Conclusion reviews how the women of *quyi* successfully navigated the liminal space between voice and body; male and female; life and imagination; words and music; and master and disciple. As a postscript, I discuss a documentary featuring Luo Yusheng that provides a fitting ending to the study. As a late twentieth-century version of Bai Niu, Luo Yusheng embodies all the qualities possessed by the women of *quyi*: mellifluous voice, androgynous stage persona, tactical intelligence, and iconic status as an innovator among both male and female performers in the city of Tianjin. The airing the documentary in 2012, on the tenth anniversary of her death, introduced Luo to a younger audience, thereby extending her legacy to a new generation.

Multiplicity of female experiences

The women of *quyi*, who began their careers in early-twentieth-century Tianjin, were unusual, and their story is important because it represents one of the many that form the mosaic of feminine cultures in China. I agree with Tani Barlow that no single study can (or should be expected to) epitomize or represent all Chinese women (1994: 253–290). Similarly, as Cahill and Hansen explain:

> No one concept of human being will embody or capture the ideals of all human beings. In order for us to think abstractly about humanity, we will continually need a plurality of models of human beings that are irreducible and hence incapable of prioritization.
>
> (2003: 14)

Hershatter raises another related issue in studying women in modern Chinese history, and concludes that the biographies of Chinese women in the twentieth century are conspicuously absent. Hershatter believes that scholars should look to the interstices between centuries, particularly between the nineteenth and twentieth centuries, in order to discover when gender seemed to matter and when it appeared to recede in importance (2007: 113, 144). This book heeds this call and addresses a period of time when gender did matter—in the interstices between the late Qing dynasty and the early Republic—when the unique convergence of historical, political, and social circumstances allowed women to appear as respectable performers on public stages. As Susan Mann explains, one of the most important overarching patterns in the transition from the nineteenth to the twentieth centuries was the movement of women toward work and study outside the home—a movement whose repercussions are still being felt (2011: xvii). Recognizing the need for a plurality of feminine models in China, and the particular importance of including working women whose life experiences have generally not been given their due (Ko and Wang 2007: 8–9), this study celebrates a particular idiosyncratic community of low-born women whose compelling stories might be perceived as one contrapuntal theme in a complex cultural fugue of Chinese female experience during the early to middle decades of the twentieth century.

Because Chinese women—especially subaltern ones—usually do not figure importantly in historical documentation, Mann and Cheng also suggest that scholars look elsewhere for the contributions and presence of women:

> [W]omen's low profile in historical documents may deceive us, masking their central place in the emotional and material lives of the men who dominate the written record. To compensate, we must pay the closest possible attention to sources where women do appear. Women are far more visible in personal, intimate, homely, or local texts than they are in texts produced by the imperial scholarly apparatus, or in formal "official" prose.
>
> (2001: 4)

In addition to these local texts, I also suggest that the performing arts provide yet another place where female contributions are manifest. In *Women Playing Men*, Jiang demonstrates how "local-opera and storytelling genres were the most direct and authentic expressions of the life experiences and imaginations of the Chinese people in their various local environments" (2009: 7), and women made substantial contributions to these art forms in the first half of the twentieth century.

Finally, I also look to the performing arts for models in interpreting issues pertaining to the status of Chinese women. The performing arts provide an opportunity to view relationships without having to peel away layers of government rhetoric or the self-conscious responses of people who are afraid to speak their true feelings for fear of government reprisal. And, according to Harris and Pease, musical performance is a particularly good place to witness how gender roles are continually being negotiated (2013: 2). As masters of androgyny and liminality, the women of *quyi* were especially skilled in navigating gender roles by capitalizing on the artistry of their musical voices and de-emphasizing their bodies in performance.

Notes

1 See n.3 of the Prologue.
2 Although this story may appear to be a political narrative in favor of the Chinese Communist revolution, communicating pro-government sentiment was not the intent of my consultants; rather, they were expressing their genuine appreciation for the way prostitute singers gained acceptance in post-1949 China. For a story about a female singer with a different way of navigating gender dynamics than the one described in this account, see Zhao (2014).
3 Sometimes Romanized as "Kuomintang," this term refers to the Nationalist Chinese Party under the leadership of General Chiang Kai-shek.
4 See Chapter 2 for a summary of *The Courtesan's Jewelbox.*
5 The exception to the paucity of biographical information on female narrators from Tianjin is the research concerning Luo Yusheng. For information about her life, repertoire, and career, see Gong (1999); Jia (2008); Liu (1983); Luo (1993); Meng and Luo (2012); Nan and Qian (1999); Tao (1983); Wu (2012); and Xue (1984). For an account in English about a female narrator who spent a good deal of her early career in Tianjin, see Zhang Cuifeng's (1985) ghostwritten autobiography.
6 For a small selection of representative scholarship in Chinese opera see Stock 2003, Li 2006, Goldstein 2007 and Jiang 2009; on gender studies see Barlow 1994, Mann and Cheng 2001, Brownell and Wasserstrom 2002, Ko and Wang 2007 and Bossler 2013; and on musicology see Zeitlin 2006 and Harris and Pease 2013.
7 For more information about the history of *quyi*, see Lawson 2011: 17–20.
8 Given the importance of liminality in performance theory, I turn to Richard Schechner's standard definition of the term for my subsequent discussions about liminality in various Chinese performance traditions.
9 Although she does not use the term metaphysical feminine, Sophie Volpp discusses the way male actors embody a kind of perfected femininity in Ming theatre (2011: 153–160).
10 While many early-twentieth-century female singers were indeed sexualized, I will argue that the women who adopted an androgynous persona became highly respected because they de-emphasized their feminine appearance. The androgyny of female singers is discussed in more detail at the end of Chapter 1.

1 The Female Voice and Body Problem

Like the body from which it emanates, the female voice is construed as both a signifier of sexual otherness and a source of sexual power, an object at once of desire and fear.

Leslie C. Dunn and Nancy A. Jones (2001: 3)

Adorno infamously claimed that phonographic recordings of female voices are problematic because a woman's singing voice requires the presence of her body (Engh 2001: 120). He believed that listening to a mechanical recording prevents the appreciation of the female voice by removing it from the body that gives it subjective meaning for the listener.[1] Adorno's claim reflects a longstanding ambivalence towards the voices and bodies of women, displayed throughout the history of musical performance.[2] As Dunn and Jones argue, "the female voice, whether it is celebrated, eroticized, demonized, ridiculed or denigrated, is always stigmatized, ideologically 'marked,' and construed as a 'problem' for the (male) social critic/auditor, who demands concern if not control" (2001: 9). And the stigma attached to the female voice is exacerbated by the presence of the female body.

This chapter will discuss what I call "the female voice and body problem," through selected examples from Western musical theater and contrasting examples from Chinese musical theater. Despite the vastly different historical and philosophical paradigms that undergird Western and Chinese musical performance, one recurring theme is the perceived need either to contain the power of the female voice and body or to eliminate female singers completely from public performance.

The female voice and body problem

Evidence of the apparent need to restrict female musicianship abounds in the ethnomusicological literature. Carol Robertson claims:

> In many cultures that purposefully use musical performance to coerce or control social status, ritual knowledge and power are believed to have

belonged to women in the distant past. At some point in ancient memory, women aborted their power or were tricked into submission by competing males. Subsequent mythical explanations are given to show why women should be excluded from the dominant power structures and why men fear and must regulate the behavior of women. In other situations, men explain that since women have such great force as birth-givers, they must be kept from other kinds of power that would give them complete control over the lives and fertility of a community.

(1989: 228)

Robertson's explanation for a universal antagonism between the sexes is pointed and provocative (see also Robert Murphy 1957, 1973),[3] and meshes well with much of the research presented in Ellen Koskoff's book *A Feminist Ethnomusicology: Writings on Music and Gender* (2014). In summarizing the relationship between feminist and musicological research over the past 40 years, Koskoff highlights the ongoing problem of a ubiquitous androcentrism that devalues women's contributions to music (Koskoff 2014: 26). Koskoff cites important ethnomusicological research that moves beyond a simple binary view of gender difference to include the role of what I would call liminal performers—those who function outside of set gender and social norms (2014: 26, 29–30).[4] She argues that women who function outside the male–female binary are often awarded certain musical freedoms unavailable to conventional female performers (26).

In exploring the reasons for universal androcentrism and the importance of liminal performers in music, I turn to Faye Dudden's concept of "the body problem," which states that female performers in public venues are consumed for their sexuality rather than appreciated for their artistry. Dudden explains:

The continuing problem of a woman in public, on the street and in the workplace, is the same as the problem of a woman on the stage: she must be there in the body. To be present in the body carries with it the inherent risk of being taken as a sexual object against one's will—in sexist deprecation, in sexual harassment, in physical assault. Theatre thus exemplifies a general problem for women in public, what we might call the "body problem."

(1994: 3)

The female body problem is intensified when a female performer sings in public, and the ambivalent responses to female voices and bodies in performance engender a complex set of cultural negotiations in both Western and Chinese musical theater. The role of liminal male and female performers in both Western and Chinese musical performances underscores the importance of showcasing the prized treble voice in an androgynous body as a way of reducing the anxiety associated with the female voice and body problem. Western theater traditionally limited, removed or contained public performances of female singers, and, after the Emperor Qianlong's ban on female public performance (Harris and Pease 2013: 2), Chinese theater generally avoided featuring female singers on public stages until the early years of the twentieth century.[5]

Replacing and containing female singers in Western music

In order to appreciate how female singers have been received in public venues, it is important to recognize some of the underlying female archetypes that produce ambivalence towards women in European and North American musical theater. Linda Phyllis Austern provides one of the most elegantly articulated discussions about the dichotomous way women were perceived in seventeenth-century English culture:

> The ambivalence implicit in this English conception about women stemmed from the Christian legacy in which Mary and Eve were seen respectively as agents of salvation and destruction, and from the Classical legacy in which women were seen as sirens capable of luring men to their deaths by their seductive voices.
>
> (1989: 420)

This dual inheritance, she explains, eventually merged into the Puritan ideological emphasis on biblical literalism (420), which placed women in a clearly subordinate position and kept women off both theatrical and liturgical stages.

The reason women were banned from participating in liturgical performances stems from the passage in 1 Corinthians 14:34, in which Paul states that women should be silent in church—a ban that was interpreted as including singing as well as speaking throughout Christian Europe for several centuries. Austern observes that pre-Civil War England was one of the European cultures

> in which the cardinal virtue of public female silence was so firmly entrenched that the soprano and alto voices of the church choir belonged exclusively to males, lest the sound of Eve's descendants lure Adam's fallen sons from their devotion to God
>
> (1996: 84).

The silencing of the female voice, and the resulting invisibility of the female body on stage, ultimately extended to all public venues, because it was believed that men who succumbed to too much feminine influence were in danger of losing their masculinity (Austern 1996: 109). Since English theater was considered an effeminizing institution (Orgel 1996: 29), attending theatrical performances threatened to "sap the virility of male spectators, the dominant and most significant faction of the audience, rendering them unfit for positions of military or civic leadership and robbing the nation of economic vitality" (Shapiro 2006: 40). For this reason, the theater was a sexually charged venue, and men were particularly at risk because of the emasculating power of the spectacle.[6] Female voices and bodies were highly restricted to remove that risk.

Androgynous solutions: Boy sopranos and castrati

One solution to maintaining the treble sound in church and the female role in theater, in both religious and theatrical venues, was the use of androgynous prepubescent males. Since the treble voice was highly desirable as a balance to the lower male ranges and served as a manifestation of angelic sound in church, the preferred solution in England had been to employ juvenile male voices in church choirs, a practice that began in the thirteenth century (Zieman 2008: 21–28). By the time of the English Renaissance, contemporary theories about gender equated boys and women in vocal range and outward physical characteristics, thus rationalizing the substitution of boys for women on the theatrical stage and in church choirs. Because boys and women were perceived to be similarly underdeveloped both morally and spiritually, they

> required adult male control and gentle guidance toward properly restrained behavior. The issue of sexual control was strongly reflected in attitudes toward musical performance, since music itself was perceived as the most powerfully sensual of the arts, and ... was regarded as an overwhelmingly feminine force unless strictly regulated.
>
> (Austern 1996: 102)

However, using young males to replace females as singers presented a challenge because of their relatively short careers as treble singers. In the seventeenth century, castrating a boy before puberty to permanently fix his voice in the treble range was seen as a viable long-term solution. Freitas explains that:

> the procedure froze him within the middle ground of the sexual hierarchy ... The castrato would have been viewed as equivalent to the boy ... Although his body would increase in size, his surgery ensured that his vital heat, and thus his physical characteristics, would remain at the less markedly masculine level of youth.
>
> (2009: 108)

The boy was transformed by surgical mutilation into

> something deemed more compelling than Nature's own creations. And yet this change did not make him alien. Rather, theater and life so thoroughly interpenetrated in this century as to make a castrato ... seem just one more avatar—if especially vivid—of the erotically boyish male.
>
> (Freitas 2009:148)

By the eighteenth century, a time when artifice dominated cultural and theatrical performances, the castrato figure was considered an embodiment of the extravagance of the age as well as a popular replacement for the female singer (148).

Castration became increasingly popular in providing treble voices for Italian opera and liturgical music in the seventeenth and eighteenth centuries. As the tradition took hold, the powerful and highly trained voice of the castrato dominated in ecclesiastical and dramatic settings. Prest explains that

> a good castrato ... offered a highly desirable combination of vocal brilliance and power, a wide vocal range, and exceptional breathing capacity. Additionally, the unearthly (i.e., unfamiliar and unusual) timbre of his voice brought to church music a "sense of asceticism and angelic asexuality."
>
> (2013: 130)

Notwithstanding the brilliant and unearthly sound of the castrato, Bartoli wonders why performers and music scholars have rarely discussed the barbarism associated with the castrato tradition (2009). Bergeron cites one particular incident in the eighteenth century in which an elaborate effort was made to avoid discussing the surgical procedure associated with castration, resembling "what we would call today an 'open secret,' a narrative practice concealing an unsavoury act in the folds of a great, culturally sanctioned alibi" (1996: 171).

Despite the apparent taboo against openly discussing castration, and the savagery of the practice,[7] the issue of castration anxiety became a central idea in late nineteenth- and twentieth-century Freudian psychoanalysis. Although an in-depth discussion of castration anxiety is well beyond the scope of this work, Barbara Creed's provocative rereading of Freud's ideas (Creed 2007: 87–166) provides insights that are pertinent to my argument about the enormous efforts expended to avoid witnessing and recognizing the central role of the female voice and body. Instead of subscribing to Freud's notion that women terrify because their genitals appear castrated, Creed argues that women's genitals terrify because they might castrate. She explains:

> Fear of the castrating mother may also help to explain the ambivalent attitude in which women are held in patriarchal societies—an attitude which is also represented in the various stereotypes of feminine evil that exist within a range of popular discourses ... My intention, however, is not to try and absorb the figure of the maternal castrator into Freud's theory of the Oedipus and castration complexes but rather to point out the inadequacy of these theories in helping us to understand the origins of patriarchy.
>
> (2007:164)

Creed's claim that women are feared as castrators aligns with many of the above-mentioned ideas about Western female singers as emasculating, siren-like seducers of hapless male victims (Austern and Naroditskaya 2006). Creed's reading also speaks to the notion of androcentrism. She explains:

> Perhaps one should conclude that acceptance of the notion of "woman as castrator" rather than "woman as castrated" is not only threatening to Freud as a man but also damaging to his theories of penis envy in women, the castration crisis and the role he assigns to the father in the transmission of culture.
>
> (2007: 121)

Creed's idea of the "femme castratice" as a requisite for removing the emasculating female voice and body by creating a female-sounding substitute[8] informs her assertion that the "threat of castration is not something enacted in the real; it is always symbolic" (160). But the castrato tradition was, indeed, real. The practice of castration had waned significantly by the nineteenth century, and the last acknowledged castrato died in 1922, at the peak of Freud's career.[9] Significantly, in both real and symbolic castration, the desire to curtail and challenge the significance of the female voice and body is highlighted.

The flip side of the barbarism associated with the castrato tradition is the appeal of an endearing, inter-gendered figure who functioned as a culturally celebrated replacement to the feared female singer. Its popularity likely stemmed from its ability to relieve gender anxiety, a dynamic which was explained by Paul Schalow (2006) in his examination of audience responses to an *onnagata* (female impersonator) in a seventeenth-century Japanese kabuki play. While the *onnagata*, who portrays female roles but does not sing, is vastly different from the seventeenth- and eighteenth-century castrato in Italian opera, both the *onnagata* and the castrato functioned as inter-gendered beings. Schalow's explanation for the audience's reaction to the androgynous *onnagata* in a particular play reveals one of the reasons for the castrato's popularity in Italian opera. By moving down the gender hierarchy to portray a woman, the *onnagata* relieved the apprehension and uneasiness associated with strict social hierarchies. In the play about Amida, the androgyny of the *onnagata* complemented the portrayal of this androgynous, Buddha-like character. Schalow explains that the response to the *onnagata* indicated "the audience's desire to transcend gender, or at least to relieve the anxieties associated with maintaining rigidly-defined gender roles ..., allow[ing] men and women alike to give up their male or female positions and prerogatives" (2006:64). Schalow goes on to explain, "the experience of being relieved of gender ... is the pleasure of the *onnagata* for the audience" (64). The same logic could be applied to the liminal, inter-gendered figure of the castrato, which provided a solution, however barbaric, to the female voice and body problem.

However, the castrato provided more than just anxiety relief, and the *onnagata* tradition once more offers some insights that may shed light on

European women's fascination with the castrato. In discussing the seventeenth- and eighteenth-century *onnagata* tradition, Laurence Kominz argues that female fans were wooed by the way *onnagata* actors devoted themselves to portraying female characters on stage, appealing to the female fans who were "essential and irreplaceable, not only in terms of box office receipts, but as judges of an actor's skill and appeal" (1997: 183). In explaining the original adulation for and continued fascination with *onnagata* by both seventeenth-century and contemporary Japanese female fans, Kominz argues that women "feel gratified and flattered that a man has taken such pains to understand and take into his own soul the feelings of women" (1997: 253). Japanese women's appreciation for the *onnagata* parallels Orgel's explanation for why lavish, feminized male clothing was designed to please seventeenth-century English gentlewomen: "women are won by imitation; what they want are versions of themselves" (1996: 87).

Although they were not imitating women, the androgynous castrati were certainly more closely aligned with women than conventional male singers by virtue of their high vocal range, which added an element of sexual attraction.[10] The popularity of castrati demonstrates their broad cultural appeal but, more critically, the act of castration reflects the enormously abusive efforts to restrict female voices and bodies.

Sirens vs. songbirds: Dichotomous archetypes and the undoing of women

Although castrati did not replace women on the opera stage, *prima donnas*, as publicly visible working artists provoked a perceived need to contain their influence on public stages. Rutherford comments that the problematic reception of female vocalists had been in evidence since (and arguably long before) the birth of opera in the early seventeenth century (2006: 33). The *prima donna* was considered a "songbird" because of her voice, but her voice also made her a seductive "siren" (36–57). Rutherford continues, "No other woman ... in this era encompassed such a range of interpretative possibilities, was both so idolized and so despised; she was, in short, a living metaphor for her sex" (34).

While the power of the female voice allowed nineteenth- and early twentieth-century *prima donnas* to achieve a level of social standing unheard of in previous generations, these women also paid a price for their adulation. Maria Malibran, a highly talented and flamboyant *prima donna*, was frequently conflated with the tragic roles she played onstage. For example, when she was rehearsing the role of Desdemona in Rossini's *Otello* at the age of 15, she was threatened with strangulation by her father and vocal teacher, Manuel Garcia, if she did not perform to his expectations. Mary Ann Smart comments:

> More striking than the cruelty of the threat is the tale's narrative force, the way it superimposes art on life [and] reads Malibran's relationship

with her father through her most famous role. It is a gesture endlessly repeated, until singers' lives begin to seem as alike as opera plots.

(1995: 171)

A similar situation occurred with Rosine Stoltz, whose personal life became the center of a controversy concerning the stability of Parisian opera. As Smart explains:

> Professional success and sexual power can be a threatening combination ... The obsessive focus on Stoltz's personal life masks a deeper historical narrative, a documentation of the Opéra's decline, which was all but inevitable by the time Stoltz made her debut in 1837, but for which she nevertheless became a scapegoat.

(1995: 175)

The practice of conflating the lives of *prima donnas* with their stage personas continued into the twentieth and twenty-first centuries. In *Demented: The World of the Opera Diva*, Ethan Mordden highlights the way opera stars have been alternately idolized and despised, as evidenced by the wild and irrational female characters they have portrayed onstage (1990: 11–12). Catherine Clément, in *Opera, or the Undoing of Women* (1988), insists on stripping away the elegant music, extravagant costumes and elaborate sets to focus on the libretti, which reveal, as Susan McClary explains, an anthropological and psychoanalytical interpretation of elite European culture that exposes the degradation of women (McClary 1988: xi).

A more recent example of the way opera continues to revel in the undoing of women is the production of Mark-Anthony Turnage's opera, *Anna Nicole*, commissioned by the Royal Opera and first performed in 2011. On the opera's website, the plot is summarized as follows:

> A small-town waitress decides to become a stripper, weds an octogenarian billionaire and becomes a Playboy model and celebrity. But as her fame grows, so does the exploitative behavior of those close to her, the intrusiveness of the media and her own dependence on drink and pills.[11]

Her life is described as both flamboyant and tragic, not unlike many of the characters of nineteenth-century operas or the *prima donnas* who portrayed them.

A related example of undoing women in American popular culture is Lady Gaga's staged performance of her own death in her music video version of "Paparazzi" in 2009 (Herbert 2010: 67–74).[12] The song has been critically acclaimed, which makes the dramatization of her death in the music video even more significant. Even though Lady Gaga cleverly and purposefully appropriates the archetype in her performance, the misogyny inherent in the dying, tragic female character endures.

Western solutions: Undone female singers and androgynous male singers

The act of undoing female performers by depicting the heroines they portray in demeaning ways lessens the power of the anxiety-producing female body and voice in public venues. As a corollary to this point, replacing female singers with androgynous male singers removes the anxiety-producing female performer from the stage; preserves the highly valued treble sound; and appears to function as a form of sexual signaling[13] for young female fans as seen the examples below. Androgynous male singers in the popular music realm—albeit not castrated—continue to charm audiences as they did in the heyday of the castrati. Feminized males, from the Beatles to male singers in contemporary indie rock bands, sing in a relatively high tessitura; avoid the female body problem by removing the female body from the stage; and tend to attract female audiences. Steven Stark explains that young women in the 1960s were passionate about the Beatles because they were able to see these androgynous singers as reflections of themselves (2005: 133), a point reminiscent of Orgel's comment about women wanting imitations of themselves (1996: 87).[14] The popularity of male androgyny may be, as Schalow says, due to the *direction* of the androgyny—from the more powerful male to the less powerful female gender (2006: 67), thereby simultaneously relieving gender anxiety for men and providing a titillating, approachable, feminized male image for women.

But what about female androgyny?[15] Although feminized males generally seem to be preferred over masculinized females in Western musical and theatrical performances, female androgyny is also celebrated in certain contexts, particularly in China. The primary reason for the popularity of female androgyny in China has been its congruence with certain cultural narratives. And yet, examples of both male and female androgyny exhibit a similar confluence of two traits: a highly esteemed treble voice housed in an androgynous body.

Excising the female singer: Selected examples from Chinese music

The female singing voice and body were both perceived differently in the Chinese performing arts than in Western theater. Confucian social dicta forbade respectable women from appearing—let alone singing or acting—in public performance, so males impersonated most female roles in public performance,[16] thereby removing the voice and body problem. The concept of female purity, or *qingbai*, was the main driving force behind segregating men and women in public venues (Jiang 2009: 60–69), so, in order to provide female roles in Chinese theater, male actors appropriated female characters, bodies, and voices to create a world of androgynous femininity to compensate for the absence of respectable female performers.[17] The female voice and body did not pose the same kind of threat in the Chinese context that they did in Western musical theatre, so the Chinese performing arts depict sexuality, female icons, and the boundaries between genders very differently than they do in the West. Susan Mann notes:

> In a culture in which sex was never coupled with sin—in which Adam and Eve had no role in the cultural or historical explanations for sexual desire and its consequences—the Chinese conviction that sexual activity is an essential part of a healthy human life softened and defused the conflicts about homoerotic desire, and about homosexual and transgendered identities, that feed homophobia and even violence in many modern cultures.
>
> (2011: xvii)

Because they are not being blamed for sexual sin, Chinese female characters are frequently portrayed more positively than the often Janus-faced female archetypes in Western musical theater. However, this does not mean there were no *femme fatales* in Chinese theater. The treatment of sexually transgressive characters in Beijing theatre during the Qing period, as discussed by Andrea Goldman, is a case in point (2012: 175–236).[18] Instead, I am arguing that the Chinese metaphysical feminine trope exists in stark contrast to many of the negative roles portrayed in Western musical theatre—a trope that was eventually appropriated by female narrators in Tianjin. Yuejin Wang recognizes what he calls a "Chinese femininity complex" in the late Qing and early Republican period (1991: 83), which is a dominant feminine undercurrent in Chinese cultural performances. He insists that an important subset of male figures in literature and in dramatic performance from that period is often seen as deficient and seeking feminine qualities, a subject I will pursue in more detail in Chapter 2.

The boundaries between the sexes in Chinese theater are much more fluid than they are in their Western counterparts. Notwithstanding the seventeenth-century European notion of a one-sex system in which genders could be created and changed from one to the other, Western performances since the seventeenth century have been constrained by more rigid conceptions about gender differences. Androgynous portrayals in Chinese theater have been particularly rich, partly because of the ancient Daoist metaphysical concepts of *yin* and *yang*, which have ultimately inspired and encouraged androgyny in the theater (Li 2006: 165). Within the body, a proper balance between *yin* and *yang*—a balance that changes throughout the life cycle for both men and women—is encouraged, suggesting a fluidity of gender characteristics (Furth 1999). Moreover, as Yi-Li Wu argues, the human body is believed to be capable of producing many forms, including a variety of genders. She explains:

> So rather than describe the Chinese doctrinal body as androgynous, which defines it in terms of possessing male and female attributes, I instead call it an infinitive body, one that serves as the basis for all human bodies, to be conjugated into male and female, young and old, robust and delicate, Southern and Northern, depending on circumstance.
>
> (2010: 232–233)

Although female actors performed in private troupes, it is important to acknowledge the way female actors were usually denied the opportunity to perform in a public theatrical or musical venue before the Republican period. Mann explains how the purity of women was one of the most important marks of respectability, particularly in nineteenth-century China. She notes, "The sex and gender system in nineteenth-century China revolved around cloistered women. Boundaries that concealed women defined the system, and the sexuality and status of every man and woman in the empire was measured in relation to those boundaries" (2011:3). Gender-bending androgyny became part and parcel of the Chinese performing arts because of limits imposed by Confucian ideals, enabled by the polysemy implied by Daoism. As a result, the effects of *qingbai* and the resulting prohibitions against mixed-gender social settings invariably demanded single-gender troupes in the theater, namely all-male troupes for public performances and all-female troupes for private, elite social gatherings.

As a result, female chastity in China highlighted the voice and body problem even more strikingly than in the West, and the cloistering of elite Chinese women was considered more necessary in public performance than in general social interactions because of the passionate emotions stimulated by the theater. As Goldstein reminds us:

> Drama was potentially dangerous for a very simple reason: it was fun. Drama appealed to the emotions, beguiling the senses with music and pageantry ... It could, and often did, attract the wrong kind of people and excite the wrong kinds of passions, and people who have too much fun are neither good subjects nor responsible officials.
>
> (2007:58)

Allowing respectable women to attend public theater—let alone act on stage—only would have exacerbated the perceived danger. It was not until the 1920s that most major urban theaters even permitted men and women to sit together (Goldstein 2007: 69). So, while European actresses were appearing on public stages by the end of the seventeenth century, female performers in late imperial China "lost ground to male players from the seventeenth to the nineteenth centuries because the Confucian sexual ideology ... dividing men and women was more seriously and determinedly carried out" (Li 2006: 51).

An androgynous solution: Metaphysical femininity and the male *dan*[19]

One of the effects of reducing the number of female actors in public performance was the emergence of the androgynous male *dan*—the most famous and beloved example of female impersonation. While banning female actors from Chinese public theater took away their physical presence and maintained Confucian sensibilities about female chastity, a powerful feminine energy remained in the androgynous performances by the male dan—an energy that intensified during the Republican period, at the apex of their popularity (Wang 2003). Removing female performers from the public sphere seemingly unleashed a surge of suppressed female energy that was rechanneled into unusually powerful feminine portrayals by the male *dan*.

This redirecting of feminine energy is similar to a concept proposed by Bruno Nettl, which states that society exhibits a kind of homeostasis by maintaining a constant amount of musical energy. Nettl argues that when some energy is channeled into a new musical system, less energy is available for the former system (1985: 20, 26). Building on that point, removing women as performers and audience members in Chinese public performance seems to have necessitated a channeling of feminine energy to the male *dan* in order to re-establish gender homeostasis in the performing arts.

In the process of redistributing gender energy, feminine portrayals gained power proportionate to the degree that women were removed from public performance. Despite its intended meaning for a postmodern world, Baudrillard's concept of a simulacrum (2010: 6) epitomizes the way the male *dan* appropriated the entire tradition of female representation, creating a "pure simulacrum" of feminine reality to supplant actual female performers—a representation that I refer to as *metaphysical femininity*.[20] Metaphysical heroines are characters with both conventional feminine qualities, such as righteousness, and conventional masculine characteristics, such as bravery. It is here, in the interstices between masculinity and femininity, that the metaphysical feminine thrived and empowered male performers. Unlike highly ambiguous European female icons, who were often seen alternatively as agents of salvation and destruction,[21] Chinese metaphysical heroines are nearly always exemplary and virtuous characters who figuratively exalted the male performers in the narrative arts (the predecessors of female narrators) in the same way they glorified the male *dan* in opera during the Republican period.

Subsequent discussions about the liminality inherent in metaphysical femininity in this and later chapters reveal a blurred area between masculinity and femininity that became a mother lode for the richly complex portrayals of metaphysical femininity in Chinese cultural performance. Consequently, male performers were keen to portray these liminal figures because they were more inspiring and interesting than conventional male or female characters. The resultant simulacrum of metaphysical femininity provides one of the most interesting examples of liminality in Chinese culture, and the androgynous male *dan* were particularly well suited to inhabit this space.

Similar to a position Judith Butler took many centuries later (1988: 521, 524–528), Chinese performers traditionally believed that gender could be portrayed convincingly through the artistry of the performer and was not dependent on the performer's biological sex. However, while Butler disavows essentialist notions regarding gender identity, Chinese performers believed in the essence of biological sex. In fact, a great transvestite performer was one who captured the sexual identity of a character, thereby becoming a member of the opposite sex through the act of skillful performance (Li 2006: 165). Until, and even during, the Republican period, the Chinese believed that playing a character of the same gender did not require the same level of artistry as cross casting (Li 2006: 30). Hence, the incentive for Chinese transvestite theater was the perceived need to maintain Confucian ideals about sexual propriety, yet the inherent Daoist belief in the fluidity of gender boundaries enabled Chinese theater to develop a rich and aesthetically satisfying tradition of androgynous performance. Such performances helped place metaphysical femininity within a cultural domain that influenced many other aspects of Chinese society, including, eventually, the world of female narrators.

Creating a metaphysical feminine voice

Like the castrati,[22] the male *dan* were inter-gendered individuals who relieved gender anxiety during the Republican period. Unlike the castrati, the male *dan* did not undergo surgical procedures to alter their voices.[23] Instead, they painstakingly created a falsetto voice that was considered to be an aesthetic representation of the female voice in the same way that their bodily movements and words were constructed to be aesthetically—and not realistically—feminine. Describing the voice of one of the most famous *dan* during the Republican era, Goldstein explains how Cheng Yanqiu constructed new ways of singing in the feminine style of a *dan*:

> Cheng Yanqiu ... [became] to many ... the most inventive and emotionally moving singer of the era. With a voice described as autumnal, plaintive, gentle, "a cloud-shrouded moon," Cheng generally sang in a lower register than was typical of *dan*; when reaching into the higher range, his voice became sharper, seemingly angry, defiant. With these vocal elements, enriched by his talent at smoothly weaving together different melody styles and sensitively varying his pacing to reflect his character's emotions, Cheng developed a mournful "new melody" and won accolades for his portrayals of tragic women.
>
> (2007: 260)

Yet even in the world of female impersonation, there was tension between the feminine voice and the body. Comparing two of the prominent female role types in Beijing opera, Goldstein connects the aural beauty of the voice of the visually bland *qingyi* (the virtuous female archetype) with the playfully seductive, visually alluring *huadan* (the coquette) (2007: 123).[24] Plays that feature the *qingyi* traditionally were about chaste marital love, and the *qingyi* character often dressed simply, moving about with unassuming poise. Goldstein explains, "A *qingyi's* artistry greatly emphasized virtuoso singing, and many argued that it was best savored with one's eyes closed, a visual indifference all the more appropriate because a virtuous woman was supposed to avoid the gaze of strangers" (2007: 123). The *huadan*, by comparison, was a flirtatious young woman who was

> colorfully dressed, with shorter, open sleeves to facilitate lively gesturing, and moving with a dancelike, alluring sway[;] a *huadan* was meant to compel visual attention and seduce the audience, speaking as much with her eyes and hands as through her song.
>
> (2007:123)

In other words, female chastity—the epitome of Chinese virtue—was *heard* optimally through the voice of the *qingyi*, where the body was minimized and the voice maximized; seduction, on the other hand, was *seen* through the visually enticing, dancing body of the *huadan*.

Popularity of the Male *Dan*

Mei Lanfang combined the *qingyi* and *huadan* role types to create the *huashan* character—a new female archetype that brought together the virtue and voice of the former with just enough of the sexual appeal of the latter to make the *huashan* respectable yet more well-rounded than any other feminine character in Beijing opera during the Republican period. This contribution, among others made by Mei and the other famous female impersonators in Republican China, made female impersonation "the greatest, most enduring, and most ubiquitous art in China," according to an essay written by the author Lu Xun in 1924 (Lu 1981: 294). Female impersonation was an artistic tour-de-force because it was an embodiment of Daoist ideals in the service of Confucian virtue, providing a clever and aesthetically pleasing solution to the voice and body problem for Chinese audiences.

David Der-wei Wang also suggests another reason for the popularity of female impersonation (2003: 140). In his analysis of two literary pieces written during the Republican period, *The Second Mother* and *Begonia*, Wang argues that the authors of these two works played upon the sympathies of Republican audiences by associating female impersonation with the theme of motherhood (2003: 133). According to Wang, both works "enchant us not because they are womanly arts as such but because they induce a specular sensation among the audiences making gender attributes appear to be transferable artifacts" (160). The portrayals of the male *dan*, imbued with a sentimentality associated with maternal love, frequently inspired "sighs and tears," evoking strong emotions from both male and female readers and operagoers (159). The political pressure to abolish female impersonation was resisted by the general populace, which relished the sentimentality of the stories.

A third reason for the popularity of the male *dan* in the late Qing and Republican periods was his sexual appeal. Because homosexual male liaisons were not as carefully scrutinized as their heterosexual counterparts, under "the guise of theatre, male courtesan culture went theoretically underground, all the while becoming a surrogate for straight erotic culture" (Wang 2003: 145). But the male *dan* was not attractive only to homosexual males; the androgyny of the male *dan* attracted heterosexual and homosexual males both. As Wang explains, female impersonators were

> trained to act like women so as to create simulacra of female beauties, and their patrons are accordingly pleased to treat them as women. This is truly a social milieu wherein life imitates art ... heterosexual and homosexual males are seen as jointly participating in an escapade in developing, or even discovering, their alternative desires.
>
> (2003: 145)

Just as Japanese women loved the *onnagata*, Chinese women appreciated female impersonators.[25] The male *dan* portrayed the loftiest examples of the metaphysical feminine, such as chaste widows; virtuous young women with the highest ideals; and wronged but righteous courtesans. Even though these metaphysical feminine archetypes were initially unavailable to female actors and did not exonerate actual women, female audience members—even when sequestered from male attendees—could vicariously appreciate the artistry of a male actor who took the time to champion women. As the legendary eighteenth-century *onnagata* Yoshizawa Ayame charmed his female audiences with his unusually sympathetic portrayal of women (Kominz 1997: 200–204), so Republican female impersonators captivated their female audiences with their positive and sensitive portrayals of female characters. Female fans could easily look up to gifted actors who served as role models and champions of feminine virtues. Hence, the androgynous male *dan* had the power to enthrall virtually every audience member, regardless of sexual orientation or gender.

Related to the popularity of the male *dan* among male and female fans was the notion of anxiety relief associated with the depiction of a third gender. Paul Schalow, whose analysis was referenced earlier in this chapter, makes a fascinating point about an *onnagata* as an androgynous figure in a seventeenth-century kabuki play about Amida. Schalow argues that cross-dressing must be condescending from male to female, since in that movement "the *powerful* embraces the *weak* in a compassionate, Buddha-like motion" (2006: 67). He further explains that the "release from gender strictures ... was allowed by the hegemonic powers only as long as the mechanism of release, the *onnagata*, maintained the hierarchy of power between superior (male) and inferior (female)" (2006: 68).

While certainly not a religious icon, the male *dan* did function as a third gender for Chinese audiences and represented the same kind of condescending gesture. His onstage portrayals epitomized idealized metaphysical femininity, and his life offstage as a male citizen gave him social standing and credibility that further validated the femininity he portrayed onstage, enabling him to become a patriarchal spokesperson for women during the Republican period.

The most notable example of the symbolic movement from male actor to female character is the role played by Mei Lanfang who, as the greatest *dan*, was a strong, highly regarded male citizen who embraced the weaker portrayals of femininity. His position as a feminized, androgynous male made him appealing to women as a sympathetic ambassador of the female sex, and made him a non-threatening example of Chinese artistry to male audience members.

The emergence of female performers

The qualities that enabled the male *dan* to be simultaneously the quintessence of tradition and the epitome of a modern Chinese citizen were initially not available to female performers. In the early years of the Republic, actresses did not portray beloved metaphysical feminine characters. Instead, they were cast to match their real-life personalities in such a way as to imply that there was no acting involved—"with real life presaged in fiction and fiction endlessly repeating the tragedies of life, until the cycle of suicide itself almost seemed impelled by the very act of its representation" (Goldstein 2007: 238). In the same way that Rosine Stoltz's personal reputation was compromised by her operatic roles in nineteenth-century France, so a Chinese actress's stage persona similarly damaged her character and social standing (Smart 1995: 175). Jin Jiang further explains,

> the public imagined the [Chinese] actress as if it were involved in a love affair with her and therefore had a claim on her sexuality and loyalty ... The public paradoxically demanded chastity from its favorite actresses as it simultaneously consumed their sexuality.
>
> (2009: 63)

Kano explains a similar dilemma encountered by Japanese actresses as Japan embraced modernity and its concomitant theatrical conventions. As in China, Japanese women had not been allowed to perform on a theatrical stage for centuries; when Japanese actresses first appeared on stage and in film, Japanese audiences (and Chinese, by extension) responded to their presence the way English audiences had first reacted to actresses in Restoration theater:

> In both instances, a tradition of using male performers of female roles was replaced by the emergence of the actress ... It seems to have been "both reactionary and subversive, questioning as well as reinforcing traditional dramatic female stereotypes"—simultaneously allowing women a voice on the public stage as well as leading to greater objectification and heightened voyeurism of the female body. The same assessment could be made about Japanese actresses after the Meiji Restoration.
>
> (Kano 2001: 8–9)

Eventually, the attitudes toward actresses and theater in China and Japan diverged. Western-influenced Japanese drama necessitated the use of actresses, but the rise of the female performer in drama and film has "never in any way undermined the time-honoured use of the traditional *onnagata* [Japanese female impersonators] ... in Kabuki" (Fujita 2006: 140).

By contrast, the influence of international feminism on the modernizing Chinese Republic changed the attitudes of many Chinese intellectuals and activists, who looked at female impersonation in traditional Chinese opera as decadent and backward, despite the public's attraction to the male *dan*.[26] Consequently, the practice was discouraged and eventually eliminated by the time the Chinese Communist Party assumed control in 1949 (Li 2006: 192–193), and female actors became the de facto performers of female roles in public theater. However, social and even State support did not allow women to develop their own agenda in theater or in lived social reality. As Yang explains, the modern category of gender in China has been "a fragile formation" and "its emergence was so overshadowed by the project of nation building that it did not develop into a category of affirmative self-identity for a women's movement led by women themselves" (1999: 36). Just as Chinese women did not participate in the creation of female archetypes in traditional theatrical performance that was dominated by the male *dan*, they also had little voice in State-imposed feminism. Nevertheless, Chinese female actors and singers were able to take advantage of the political climate that favored female actors playing female (and even male) roles[27] and build on the foundation created by the great male *dan* performers, who had encouraged the creation of new plays about female protagonists and rendered both repertoire and acting techniques to be more sympathetic to women (Jiang 2009: 34).

The social activism of the male *dan* also helped initiate changes that allowed female performers to claim their voices. Cheng Yanqiu, like Mei Lanfang, parlayed his popularity as a female impersonator into the political realm. Goldstein explains: "Cheng could ... do something that actresses in his day found extremely difficult: he could use the roles of women to express social protest while staying relatively aloof from sexual associations" (2007: 262). Like Western divas such as Angelica Catalini, Adelina Patti, and Nellie Melba, who signaled to women "the possibilities of 'voice' in every sense" (Rutherford: 15–18, 276), the great female impersonators in Chinese opera inspired broad social change for female performers. Several different groups of female performers were influenced by the modern political values championed by outspoken female impersonators such as Cheng Yanqiu. Four of these groups are discussed in this chapter: Western-style actresses, *Yue* women's opera actresses, prostitute singers, and the female narrators of Tianjin *quyi*.

Western-style actresses

Western-style actresses engendered the most anxiety-producing response of all the Chinese female performers in the early years of the Republic. When an actress stepped on to the stage or appeared on screen, she assumed a power normally unavailable to women bound by traditional Confucian social norms. Schalow explains that in seventeenth-century Kabuki theater, the "woman-dressed-as-man is a *usurping* motion, and the act of *insubordination* in a Confucian context where 'station' ... was the central political fact of life" (2006: 67–68). In the case of the Chinese actresses in Western-style theater, however, the most insidious examples of insubordination occurred when women played female roles. The incendiary combination of the body problem with the increased power of assuming a masculinized position by being on a public stage violated the Confucian concept of female chastity. Opera audiences were accustomed to seeing a carefully constructed femininity on a male body, completely cloaked in ornate but modest clothing and thick, theatrical makeup. When actresses began to assume female roles on modern stages outside the conventional operatic tradition, they dressed in realistic, modern clothing and makeup and portrayed roles that reflected issues confronting citizens of the modern Republic in a broader, globalized setting. While these newer roles aligned with modernist sensibilities, the traditional opera-going public was not ready for the transition.

The tragic story of Chinese movie actress Ruan Lingyu underscores the crisis experienced by Western-style female actors in Republican China. In 1935, Ruan committed suicide shortly after starring in a film about another actress who had been driven to suicide by innuendo only a year earlier. As a straight-cast actor in the Western tradition, Ruan and other female actors were given roles that matched their real-life personalities in order to imply that no acting was involved. Western-style actresses were neither protected by elaborate makeup and costumes nor exonerated by the metaphysical feminine roles that helped validate the male *dan*. While female impersonators gained legitimacy and prestige by differentiating their onstage roles as icons of femininity from their offstage lives as male citizens, it was impossible for Western-style actresses to separate themselves from their stage personae in the early and middle decades of the Republican period.

Women portraying female roles in front of mixed audiences were subversive and rebellious figures because the presence of the female body invariably produced anxiety, thereby destabilizing and sabotaging all other semblances of male power. And if a female actor was especially attractive, the anxiety increased dramatically, placing her in what I refer to as the *danger zone*—a place in which a female performer is consumed for her sexuality rather than appreciated for her artistry. Female performers in the danger zone, such as these early Western-style actresses, were unable to perform as artists rather than as sexual objects—an opportunity that was available to other female performers who were able to assume a more androgynous persona.

Yue women's opera actresses

One of the most interesting venues that featured androgynous portrayals was the all-female *Yue* women's opera, and female patrons were its enthusiastic and devoted fans (Jiang 2009: 115). Jiang's pioneering research on *Yue* women's opera highlights an operatic tradition that changed from an all-male into an all-female genre between the 1930s and the 1980s in urban Shanghai. In response to the enthusiastic female reception of *Yue* women's opera, *Yue* opera actresses reformed its rural, all-male antecedent to an urban, all-female form that emphasized love dramas, archetypes, and models that were congruent with the nationalistic and feminist ideals of the Republic. Jiang's work emphasizes a trend in Chinese society in which women took charge of their own feminine representation, changing stories and images to fit the emerging Chinese feminism of the day. *Yue* women's opera is a fascinating account of the way women used theater to control their lives and public image for about 50 years during the twentieth century (Jiang 2009: 244–256).

Although *Yue* opera actresses initially experienced the same kinds of accusations of sexual impropriety that led to Ruan's death, they eventually overcame this denunciation and became known as advocates of women's rights (Jiang 2009: 172). The sensitive male scholar, who represented the stock-in-trade icon of *Yue* opera, was, according to Wang Yuejin, best played by a woman because only a female actor seemed able to portray the tenderness required by the female *sheng* role type—the female cross-dressed equivalent of the male *dan* (1991: 85). Wang argues that having women impersonate men "created a theatrical illusion that [stood] in for an illusion of reality: desirable male prototypes fit for such romantic slots … [were] feminized men. These cultural praxes have created an ingrained aesthetic taste in Chinese audiences for feminine male icons" (1991: 85).

By performing the female *sheng*, female actors were able to avail themselves of the power of androgyny through highly feminized male impersonation, resulting in an elevated form of metaphysical masculinity. Like the Japanese female audiences who adore the *otokoyaku* (male impersonators) of the Takarazuka Revue, female fans of *Yue* opera were passionately in favor of the female *sheng*. Critics, however, were opposed to the unrestrained public expression of adoration for actresses, as it allegedly conflicted with the ideology of nation building (Jiang 2009: 255). In contrast to the Takarazuka Revue, which continues to thrive today in Japan, the *Yue* opera began to decline in the 1980s. Male criticism of its perceived inferiority to Beijing opera and a growing awareness of its anachronism ultimately drove female audience members to patronize other forms of entertainment.[28] Even though the voice and body problem was not nearly as acute as it was with Western-style actresses, *Yue* women's opera ultimately could not compete with other more conventional operatic forms (Jiang 2009: 259).

Prostitute singers of *quyi*

Prostitute singers were also part of the musical scene in Republican China. These singers had been active for centuries, and Judith Zeitlin's research on Chinese courtesan culture in the seventeenth century[29] raises issues that are relevant to the present discussion about female voices and bodies. Courtesans in the late Ming period inhabited a society—albeit private and available only to educated literati and other courtesans—in which vocal artistry out-ranked acting. According to Zeitlin, seventeenth-century courtesans privi-leged poetry over song and favored singing over acting of any kind (2006: 78). Their continuum of artistic preferences demonstrates that cognitive literary pursuits ranked highest because of the "supreme valuation of the written word and the exaltation of literary authorship in China," where the most distinguished courtesans wrote verse preserved on paper (Zeitlin 2006: 78). "Pure singing" (without acting) was next in importance because it gave voice to written poetry, emphasized the aural over the visual, and minimized the body. The ability to write poetry, followed by the ability to render it musi-cally, was favored in a culture where women were highly cognizant of activi-ties that took attention away from their status as courtesans and towards their cognitive and artistic pursuits—activities that provided them with the most dignity. Acting, on the other hand, was least favored because of its greater reliance on the body, and because it purportedly lacked the exultation of literature or pure singing.

The same cultural stereotypes about voice and body also operated among prostitute singers during the Republican period. All female singers, including impersonators, earned the most respect when the erotic aspect of their sexual-ity was minimized and the power of their voices was maximized. However, for women trapped by prostitution, capitalizing on the allure of the female body was the entry into the singing profession, even though their eventual success as artists depended on their vocal talent. Hershatter explains the economic problems faced by prostitutes in the early years of the Republic of China:

> The paths by which these women arrived at this trade are unclear, since no record survives in their own words. The conventional wisdom among their working-class neighbors is that they were tricked or kidnapped from their homes and sold into brothels. Given the limited job options for women, undoubtedly economic need played a larger role than is acknowledged retrospectively ... Which type of work a woman did had a great deal to do with luck and connections, and very little to do with personal choice.
>
> (1986: 190–191)

Consequently, prostitutes generally were not in a position to find respected or profitable work (Hershatter 1986: 208). However, for the few women like

Tan and Du, whose stories were told in the Introduction, *quyi* became a rare opportunity for the voice to trump the body, enabling social mobility for singing narrators in an otherwise dismal market for underclass female workers in Tianjin.

The women of *quyi*

Concomitant with the successful careers of performers like Tan and Du, the time was also right for the triumph of other female narrators to win control of their voices without having to suffer from the taint of prostitution. In discovering how the women of *quyi* established themselves successfully as artists in a world that had been hostile to female performers, it is important to see what made them both similar to and different from other groups of women. Like the vocally gifted prostitute singers, the women of *quyi* were able to benefit from singing stories about metaphysical heroines. Unlike the prostitute singers, the women of *quyi* were considered working-class artists, like the actresses of *Yue* opera. Unlike their *Yue* opera counterparts, the women of *quyi* were storytellers, not actresses, so they did not have to portray male or female roles and were therefore protected from the practice of conflating roles with personal character. Instead of being associated with the negative qualities of the heroines in Western-style theater, the androgynous women of *quyi* were imbued with all the positive attributes of their metaphysical heroines (Rebollo-Sborgi 2001: 259–264). One might say that the women of

Figure 1.1 Female narrator singing with an ensemble
Chiho Nishiwaka/Oxford Designers & Illustrators

quyi, like the male *dan* and the male narrators who came before them, became "gilt" by association with their metaphysical heroines. For this reason, *quyi* lyrics about metaphysical feminine icons exalted the women of *quyi*, including the prostitute singers, whereas theatrical scripts about true-to-life female characters stigmatized actresses like Ruan Lingyu. The women of *quyi*, unlike Yue opera actors and prostitute singers, appealed to both male and female audiences as well as to the modernist sensibilities of the Republic. Finally, whereas prostitute singers and female actors were hired and strictly controlled by brothels or troupes, female narrative performers had much more freedom to choose their repertoire, accompanists, and performance venues. These female narrative artists were able to transcend their lowborn station by profiting from their androgynous role as narrators and the metaphysical feminine content of the stories.

The power of the female voice

The novelty of the female voice in a respectable performance venue was far and away the most important factor in allowing the women of *quyi* to take over narrative genres that had previously been dominated by male singers (Xue 1985b). The stated preferences of seventeenth-century courtesan singers for pure singing over acting and the connection between voice and morality in the *qingyi* role type underscore the power of the feminine voice. By inhabiting the liminal space where feminine sexuality is acknowledged without being considered erotic, female narrators were able to achieve that balance better than most other female performers. Even though the carefully constructed falsetto voice of the male *dan* had been considered aesthetically pleasing to operagoers, especially during the Republican period, the sound of the natural female voice was particularly enchanting because of its newness. Its absence from reputable public performances only heightened its positive reception in the Republican period—a subject that will be explored in more detail in Chapter 3.

De-emphasizing the body: Wang, Luo, and Shi

A corollary to the significance of the natural female singing voice in *quyi* was the purposeful de-emphasis of the female body, which was a calculated move by female narrators such as Wang Yubao (1926–); Luo Yusheng (1914–2002); and Shi Huiru (1923–1967).[30] Prostitutes who sang on public stages in Republican China were unequivocally erotic, as was expected by performers and audience members, but female narrative singers wanted to be considered as artists (Xue 1985b). Accordingly, successful female narrative singers who de-emphasized their feminine appearance were relatively unaffected by the danger zone, unlike performers like Ruan, who was consumed voyeuristically rather than respected for her dramatic talent. To become a true female artist in the *quyi* tradition, a performer had to have an exceptional voice, and audiences seemed to focus best on the voice when the female body did not distract them.

Wang Yubao serves as a fascinating example of a female actor who successfully de-emphasized her sexuality. A famous singer of the narrative genre known as Tianjin Popular Tunes (Lawson 2011: 59–76), Wang first began singing alongside her father, Wang Zhenqing, an amateur performer of the genre. In the 1930s, the father-daughter team sang at teahouses and small theaters throughout the city in order to earn extra money for the family. His paternal presence on the stage protected her from the possibility of the untoward gossip that was often aimed at female performers in a public venue, enabling audiences to focus on her vocal artistry rather than her sexuality.[31] Once she was established as one of the greatest narrative singers in Tianjin and her dignity assured by her father's initial presence, she was able to perform apart from her father, unsullied by the sexual associations that plagued performers like Ruan Lingyu. The following comment by Dunn and Jones explains the power of the female voice for Wang Yubao and the women of *quyi* when the female body is de-emphasized: "[Female singers] … reveal the existence of expressive arenas—some traditionally established, others newly created—in which feminine vocality possesses both cultural authority and creative force" (2001: 10). Indeed, feminine vocality surpassed male singers of *quyi*, revealing a new vocal and creative authority that eclipsed the body problem.

Like Wang Yubao, Luo Yusheng, whose formidable talent will be discussed in Chapter 3, was careful to accentuate her vocal gifts by consciously downplaying her makeup and clothing. One consultant explained that by the 1930s, when Luo was still young, she was careful to portray an unadorned yet dignified look when performing. One performer notes,

> she used very little makeup, wore simple clothes in either black or white, and pulled back her hair with a blue clip. She purposely did not try to dress up. Audiences appreciated this simplicity because they could focus on her artistry more clearly.
>
> (Lu 1991)

A consummate singer, Luo set the highest standards for her female contemporaries and for subsequent generations, and her simple stage demeanor was a significant part of her legacy (Lu 1991).

In addition to her exceptional voice and de-emphasized feminine stage appearance, Luo also cultivated a personality that was calculated to be different from other women. The same performer explains:

> Luo was unlike other women because she wasn't weak, shy, prone-to-tears, or "kind-hearted"—in a conventionally feminine kind of way. She came from a difficult background as an adopted child who endured physical and mental torment as she tried to perform to her father's expectations. She eventually developed a forthright, straightforward manner as

a result of her upbringing, setting her apart from other male and female performers.

(Lu 1991)

A gifted vocalist who was also a shrewd and business-savvy performer, Luo not only weathered every political change in the twentieth century, but thrived amid these changes. When asked about how Luo compared to her male colleagues, the same performer remarked that "Luo surpassed most men. She didn't apologize or defer to others because she was such a commanding individual" (Lu 1991). Luo believed that obsequious behavior was not befitting a strong person, and while the informant greatly admired Luo's forthright approach to life, she said that she simply could not emulate all of Luo's characteristics. Luo was exceptional for her combination of powerful voice, androgynous persona, and her fostering of a strong, unyielding, "masculine" personality that enabled her to assume leadership positions both in and outside of the *quyi* community (Xue 1984: 92–101).

The most dramatic example of the power of the female voice eclipsing the body was Shi Huiru, a singer known as one of the least attractive of the early Republican female performers. As the preeminent singer of the Tambourine Drumsong (*Danxiar*), Shi was remembered as being especially homely (*tebie nankan*), and audiences were cautioned to cover their eyes when listening to her live performances (Xue 1991). While this instruction might initially appear cruel, her homeliness actually contributed to an androgynous persona; it moved her well out of the danger zone, allowing her to be appreciated for her vocal skills and ennobled by a metaphysical femininity that was itself traditionally androgynous. Her popularity reinforces the triumph of the voice over the body, and she was aided by the fact that Chinese audiences were accustomed to averting their gaze when listening to singing Goldstein (2007: 123) states that the sound of the virtuous, chaste *qingyi* role type in early twentieth-century Beijing opera was best appreciated with one's eyes closed. As a consequence, audiences could reason that Shi's virtuosity was enhanced in a similar manner—by savoring the sound without visual interference in order to maximize acoustical and aesthetic enjoyment— resulting in the right balance between voice and body that allowed Shi to be appreciated as an artist.

Shi's signature piece was *The Courtesan's Jewel Box* (Pian 2011: 314–325),[32] which endeared Shi to her audiences partly because of the nobility of the female protagonist. Similar to the way audiences listened to the voice of a *qingyi* with their eyes closed, *quyi* audiences focused on the beauty of Shi's voice, which was further enhanced by lyrics that extolled the virtues of a metaphysical feminine icon. Shi's voice was so remarkable that years after her death, Liu Xiumei, a young student who wanted to study Tambourine Drumsong in the late 1960s, opted against studying with a couple of living master teachers of the genre and instead adopted Shi as her posthumous master (Liu 1985). During her years as a student in the late 1960s and early 1970s, Liu painstakingly listened to tape recordings of Shi every day while training to imitate Shi's superior vocal style.

The triumph of voice over body

Shi, Luo, and Wang, as well as Tan and Du, were only a handful of the female singers of *quyi* in early twentieth-century Tianjin (Xue 1985a), but their achievements heralded a new kind of reception for female performers in Tianjin. A combination of their exceptional voices, melodic vocal style, androgynous personae, de-emphasized bodies, and lyrics featuring metaphysical femininity enabled these women of *quyi* to find the optimal liminal space on the gender continuum, successfully circumventing the voice and body problems that vexed their colleagues in theater and opera. The female voice's ability to supersede the body recalls a comment made about the power of the female voice in Western opera by Abbate: "opera remains the one spectacle in which conventional physical beauty counts for next to nothing" (1995: 225). Unlike the male *dan*, whose performance tradition was at odds with the political goals of the modernizing nation, the women of *quyi* were able to take full advantage of their position as modern women, presenting their highly valued treble voices in androgynous bodies and thereby providing a solution to the voice and body problem.

Notes

1 See Engh (2001) for a nuanced interpretation of Adorno's claim.
2 The literature on the problematic nature of the female voice for European audiences is vast. Three particularly excellent sources that expound upon this topic include Austern (1989); Heller (2003); and Rutherford (2006).
3 Creed (1993: 16–30, 166) also addresses myths about an archaic maternal figure as they relate to the concept of the monstrous feminine within horror films, indicating a similar antagonism between the sexes.
4 I also argue that the women of *quyi* are liminal performers because of their androgyny and because of their roles as storytellers, singers, and social agents, which will be discussed in greater detail throughout the rest of the book.
5 Female impersonation was a popular solution to replacing female performers on public stages. See Zeitlin 2014: 28 (n4) for a brief discussion about the waxing and waning of cross-dressing for male and female actors in Chinese theater from the mid Qing period through the present day.
6 Throughout the sixteenth and seventeenth centuries, European thinking was influenced by the idea of the one-sex system—a system that stipulated that men and women were two forms of a single body, with men as the superior version. Women were considered especially dangerous because they had the power to subvert the system. Austern explains, "The sixteenth and early seventeenth centuries did not recognize the clear, enduring genetic distinctions between the sexes that inform our own attitudes. Instead, based on longstanding ideas of developmental physiology, the female was considered an incomplete, imperfect male, lacking only heat, from the moment of conception onward that would transform her into the superior sex. The actual physical metamorphosis from female to male had

been documented by late-Renaissance physicians, which meant, as certain English Puritan divines warned, that the opposite, less natural transformation remained frighteningly possible throughout life if a man should behave in an inappropriately effeminate fashion" (1996: 85).

7 The last known castrato, Alessandro Moreschi, died in 1922.

8 Bartoli points out there was an untold number of boys castrated each year during the seventeenth and eighteenth centuries, and the majority of them did not achieve stardom—thus, the title of *Sacrificium* for her DVD (2009).

9 See n7.

10 See Prest (2006: 135–136) for a brief discussion about the reasons why castrati were attractive to female audience members. Castrati in fact never or rarely portrayed women on stage, more often taking male roles. But the phenomenon arose in the sixteenth century as a solution to the prohibition against women singing in church, and the move to the stage is a continuation of men's voices taking the place of women's.

11 www.roh.org.uk/productions/anna-nicole-by-richard-jones, accessed February 11, 2015.

12 www.youtube.com/watch?v=QlGcICNbdtw, accessed February 12, 2015.

13 One might conceivably argue that androgynous male singers are an example of the kind of sexual signaling discussed by Miller (2000: 338–344).

14 Stark argues that female fans were captivated by the Beatles' androgynous appearance, romantic lyrics, egalitarian group dynamic, and conscious imitation of girl groups, all of which combined to endear the Beatles to young female audiences (2005: 130–137). Moreover, Gould asserts that the media only enhanced the female-friendly messages of the Beatles, enabling large masses of young women to become more aware of one another and providing an environment for female solidarity and assertiveness (2007: 184).

15 Schalow argues that the direction from female to male implies insubordination, which would have been intolerable for seventeenth-century Japanese audiences (2006: 67). Although masculinized women would appear to go counter to the gender-relieving movement from male to female androgyny, there are certain interesting cases in which masculinized women have assumed important cultural roles. Chapter 2 outlines some examples of female androgyny.

16 Female performers from the underclass did perform in public, however. Sommer (2000) and Yeh (2006) both discuss the role of subaltern female performers in the late Qing period.

17 See Chapter 2 for examples of metaphysical femininity in *quyi* texts.

18 I am grateful to Margaret Wan for pointing out this source.

19 Much of the following material was previously published in my "Bai Niu and the Women of *Quyi*: Appropriating Metaphysical Femininity and Reclaiming the Feminine Voice in Republican China," *Modern Chinese Literature and Culture*, vol. 26 (1) (Spring, 2014): 41–72. It is published here with permission from the editor of *Modern Chinese Literature and Culture*.

20 See my discussion of metaphysical femininity in the Introduction.

21 In addition to the examples of ambiguous Western female icons listed at the beginning of this chapter, see also Austern and Naroditskaya (2006).

22 Although the *onnagata* is also an inter-gendered being—and the crux of Schalow's argument about gender relief—the *onnagata* does not sing, so the issue of creating feminine vocality is irrelevant in Kabuki.

23 See David Derwei Wang's explanation of how a feminine-sounding voice was achieved by the male *dan* (2003: 135).

24 See Wichmann (1991: 7–12) for more information about role types in Beijing opera.

25 See Goldstein (2007: 122, 127, 244–245) for information about female attraction to the male *dan*.
26 While the *onnagata* tradition was questioned for similar reasons, there was never enough support to ban female impersonation in Kabuki theater.
27 For a discussion about the differences between male and female androgyny in Chinese opera, see Li (2006: 193–197).
28 Ma (2015: 136–137) also cites reasons of insolvency for the genre's waning support in the second half of the twentieth century. I am grateful to Margaret Wan for leading me to this source.
29 More about the courtesan as a heroine follows in the next chapter.
30 See n5 in the Introduction for a list of sources about Luo Yusheng. As mentioned, information about other female narrators is scarce. See Sun (2008); An (2009); Zhou (2010); Chen (2013); and Gang (2008) for a few sources that discuss the musical and poetic contributions of Wang Yubao; and Luo (2009) and Xiao (2007) for a couple of sources that briefly mention the artistry and pedagogy of Shi Huiru.
31 Like Wang Yubao, the legendary Egyptian singer Umm Kulthūm also benefitted from her father's intervention. Her career began when she was a child, accompanying her father as he performed at weddings and social gatherings (Danielson 1997: 30). Like Wang Yubao, Umm Kulthūm was popular as a young singer and her father was concerned about risking his daughter's reputation by allowing her to perform before public audiences. While Wang's father solved the body problem by performing on stage next to her to prevent possible gossip, Umm Kulthūm's father required that she dress in boy's clothing and Bedouin head-covering. For more information about the way Umm Kulthūm was protected by her father, see Danielson 1997: 30–52.
32 *The Courtesan's Jewelbox* (Dushiniang) is the piece about the virtuous but tragic courtesan discussed in Chapter 2 and in the case studies recounted in this chapter.

2 Literary Voices
Metaphysical Heroines

*It is interesting to note how persistent is the Chinese poetic convention of a
male poet figured in his own poems as a sentimental woman.*

Wang Yuejin (1991: 83)

The notion of *qingbai* dictated the segregation of men and women in public
venues, and, ideally, male actors played metaphysical female roles.[1] However,
the intimate relationship between the stage and the page in Chinese culture
also meant that Chinese writers in general, and librettists in particular, were
proficient in creating metaphysical feminine characters. The literary contributions of writers who developed metaphysical heroines served to enrich this
cultural archetype, particularly in *quyi* texts. The corpus of metaphysical
heroines in narrative libretti represents a literary androgyny—a male appro-
priation of feminized characters, metaphors, and associations that embody
the idealized perfection of metaphysical femininity. The resulting exemplary
metaphysical female characters are particularly evident in the narrative literature written by male authors and staged by male performers in the late
Qing dynasty and the early Republic.

This chapter will discuss five textual examples that represent a wide range
of metaphysical feminine attributes in *quyi* texts popular in Tianjin during
the 1980s and 1990s, including: (1) extreme talent, (2) intelligence in the service of virtue, (3) righteous indignation, (4) honorable self-sacrifice, and (5)
tragic ill-treatment. While the historical contexts and literary styles of these
examples are quite different, I have highlighted these five texts because, with
the exception of the second example, their strong metaphysical heroines were
brought to life by the voices of female narrators. The women of *quyi* co-opted
the metaphysical heroines made popular by male singers and then built upon
cherished metaphysical feminine icons to legitimize their images as female
performers in a world that had been hostile to women on public stages.
The ability of these singing narrators to benefit from metaphysical feminine
imagery is demonstrated most convincingly by the story of Bai Niu, a heroine
with an extraordinary voice.[2]

Metaphysical heroines

Extreme talent: "Bai Niu Tells a Story"

> *Whence comes this marvelous tune, sung in pristine voice?*
> *It emanates from the banks of the Great Lake in Jinan and lingers like a*
>   *fragrance.*
> *Lao Can records the magical performance*
> *Of the purest and most perfect voice.*
> *Throughout history, among all storytellers of legendary fame,*
> *None surpasses the elegant rhymes and breathtaking melodies of Bai Niu,*
> *Whose haunting song lingers after nine days, enchanting countless souls.*
>   (Zhu 1985:149)

The Chinese penchant for adapting famous literary stories for narrative performance is demonstrated by acclaimed Tianjin *quyi* author Zhu Xueying
(1985) in *Bai Niu shuoshu* ("Bai Niu Tells a Story"), a narrative poem about
the legendary performance by a young female singer who famously appeared
in the second chapter of Liu E's 1907 novel, *Lao Can youji*. Liu E's account
of the young woman is remarkable for its hyperbolic celebration of her
voice, and Zhu Xueying's later *quyi* version of the story further exalts and
venerates the young girl's vocal powers. Unlike most other *quyi* texts, which
tell an actual story with multiple characters, a plot, and a moral, Zhu's
127-line poem describes the performance venue, the girl's mesmerizing vocal
talent, and the dumbstruck audience members. Amidst the usual clamor
of a local teahouse, Bai Niu's voice captivates and transfixes her audience,
which represents a wide swath of society, from high-ranking officials and
educated scholars to local fishermen and market peddlers, causing them to
ponder questions about artistry, divinely inspired talent, and immortality.
This narrative poem, written by a respected Tianjin author for a Tianjin *quyi*
performer,[3] is about the power of a young woman's voice.[4]

Liu E's earlier account of Bai Niu is part of a well-received novel about
the end of the Qing dynasty, and the apotheosis of the young storyteller
marks the beginning of the glory days of the women of *quyi*—a period in
which actual female narrators began to take the stage as legitimate and
respected performers in north China, particularly in the city of Tianjin.
Even before the publication of Liu E's novel in 1907, some female narrators in Tianjin had begun to appropriate the urban storytelling tradition
from their male counterparts and established themselves as respected artists in the teahouses and theaters of Tianjin (Xue 1985a). After its ascent
in the early years of the twentieth century, the era of female storytelling
in Tianjin spanned the next eight decades, its heyday coinciding with
the tumultuous years of the Republic and the beginning of the People's
Republic. In 1985, the young singer appeared once again in *quyi* author
Zhu's "Bai Niu Tells a Story," where Bai Niu is reintroduced as the female

character who had already inspired a generation of female narrative singers in Tianjin.[5] The women of *quyi* experienced the rise and decline of their artistic tradition between the two literary accounts of the young singer's stunning performance.

Bai Niu became a kind of patron saint for the women of *quyi*, who achieved a level of renown unlike any other female performers in Republican China. Since Zhu's expanded narrative piece better informs the subsequent discussion about female singers—their voices, stories, singing styles, and interactions with one another within a community of primarily women—Zhu's narrative poem serves as an excellent representation of the legendary singer's performance. My italicized translation of Zhu's poem follows in its entirety, punctuated throughout by my explanations and commentary.[6]

After the opening verse cited previously, the story proper begins as Lao Can, the narrator, wonders about the unusual excitement over a storyteller in the small village he is visiting. The following second section about his bemusement is lengthy, as if to reinforce the extraordinary nature of the performance he is about to describe to the audience:

On the banks of Jinan's Daming Lake there is a teahouse,
Posted on the front door is an advertisement whose ink is not yet dry.
All that is written is "Bai Niu Tells a Story,"
And connoisseurs from all around are lured into attending.
Among those who read the advertisement is an itinerant doctor
Known as Lao Can—a man of about fifty years.
He has only been in Jinan for two or three days
When he encounters something curious and puzzling.
Whether in the lane, on a street corner, in a teahouse or wine parlor,
By the side of the road, at the water's edge, or on the banks of the lake.
All extol Bai Niu's talent in telling a story,
On this point everyone agrees—they are all of one voice.
How strange it is that a drumsinger could be so remarkable,
Why is every villager consumed by this madness?
For this reason Lao Can has come to the teahouse this day,
He wants to see for himself who Bai Niu truly is.
Arriving at the teahouse, it is still early,
With two hours before the performance.
Looking around, all the seats are filled by people from far and near,
All he wants is a place to sit, but there aren't any places left.
With no other alternative, he has to hand over some money for a seat,
In order to find a spare wooden stool.
The whole place is filled with noisy chatter,
People are talking about everything from old news to the current gossip.
In the audience there are shopkeepers and scholars,
High government officials and commoners from the marketplace.

After this long wait, Lao Can finally hears a performer whom he assumes to be Bai Niu, and is deeply impressed by her clear voice, excellent diction, and storytelling ability. However, a savvy, well-educated connoisseur nearby corrects another who shares Lao Can's misunderstanding—this first performer was actually Hei Niu, Bai Niu's protégée—and the connoisseur extols Bai Niu for her superior abilities, adding another level of anticipation for Bai Niu's upcoming performance. The distinction between *hei* (black) and *bai* (white), reflected in their names, reveals the magnitude of difference in their performances.

> *After waiting for so long, Lao Can is restless and impatient,*
> *Finally, the drumsinger emerges from backstage.*
> *To his surprise, an innocent, young girl appears*
> *And begins to sing in a clear voice to the accompaniment of the sanxian and drum.*[7]
> *As she sings, her voice is mellifluous and her lyrics clear and distinct,*
> *Like an oriole ascending from a valley or a young swallow returning to the forest.*
> *Remarkably, she is the only performer,*
> *Yet she is able to expound upon good and evil, old and new, carefully describing all the different characters with feeling, accuracy, and vividness.*
> *At this moment the young girl leaves the stage and everyone begins to chatter once again,*
> *It is even much more clamorous than before.*
> *In the midst of the talking, laughing, and hawking,*
> *Lao Can overhears comments at the neighboring table about the girl who has just performed.*
> *One says, "This young girl sings very well,*
> *I suppose she must be Bai Niu herself?"*
> *Another laughs, repeatedly gesturing with his hand to the contrary,*
> *He speaks in a refined and scholarly tone:*
> *"She is not Bai Niu, but is called Hei Niu,*
> *Sir, you are oblivious, unable to distinguish between black and white.*
> *Everything Hei Niu can do has been taught to her by Bai Niu,*
> *Hei Niu's skills are a mere pittance compared to Bai Niu's artistry.*
> *One can speak about Hei Niu's abilities,*
> *Whereas it is difficult to fathom Bai Niu's talent.*
> *One simply cannot express it in words but must sense it,*
> *In order to differentiate between the two, you must listen to Bai Niu to know the truth."*
> *After saying this, the gentleman pauses and exclaims:*
> *"Wait and see if this is true, Bai Niu is now ready to perform."*

The entire first half of the poem is spent preparing the audience (and readers) for what is to follow. When Bai Niu finally does appear, it seems as though the atmosphere has changed. What was before simply a room in a teahouse becomes the site of a transformative experience where Bai Niu, the featured storyteller in the performance, eclipses everything that has happened thus far.

> *The stage appears bright in front of Lao Can's eyes,*
> *After a moment's pause, the entire stage is resplendent, like the coming of*
>   *spring.*
> *With great poise, Bai Niu ascends the stage with deliberate steps.*
> *As she looks at the audience with sparkling eyes, all are quiet. Not even a*
>   *sparrow's peep could be heard.*
> *All listen aptly as though they are awaiting a military dispatch from an*
>   *empress.*
> *Bemused, Lao Can asks himself the question,*
> *How many times have I ever witnessed something like this?*

In the only place in the poem in which her physical appearance is mentioned, Bai Niu is described as young and simply but elegantly dressed as she ascends the stage in front of a hushed and awestruck audience. Interestingly, both Liu E's original account and Zhu's *quyi* poem emphasize Bai Niu's vocal prowess and minimize her physical appearance. This emphasis on her voice and sexual innocence is especially noteworthy since female performers on public stages are often associated with prostitution, when the public appearance of the female body creates what Dudden refers to as the body problem (1994: 2–3)—a point discussed in Chapter 1. However, the description of Bai Niu's bodily presence is relegated to this one innocuous passage, whereas the description of her superhuman vocal abilities dominates the rest of the poem, offering a fascinating portrayal of feminine vocality and pulchritude devoid of erotic sexual connotations.

> *Looking closely at the young woman, she is no more than eighteen or*
>   *nineteen years old,*
> *She wears an elegant but simple skirt,*
> *Without makeup, she looks neither plain nor seductive*
> *And appears neither unsophisticated nor poor.*
>   *Her countenance floats upward like a lotus in a pond or like poplars and*
>   *willows moving in a gentle breeze;*
>   *Her pure and untainted appearance is reminiscent of a star-studded sky,*
>   *illuminated by a bright moon.*
> *As the audience reverentially awaits her performance,*
> *Each one carefully looks at the stage in breathless anticipation of hearing*
>   *her talent.*

After several passages of building anticipation, Bai Niu begins her performance by playing a drum and clapper introduction with accompaniment by a single *sanxian* player. The following references to the "six pitches" and "five tones" denote principles from early Chinese music cosmology as a way of further elevating her art form to a level of greatness.[8]

> *There she is, lightly playing the drum and clappers, creating a clear and*
>   *crisp sound.*
> *Seemingly without effort, she joyfully performs music that is pleasing to*
>   *the ear and heart.*
> *The two strips of the metal clappers sound "ding dang dang," creating the*
>   *six pitches*
> *As the drum plays the carefully executed rhythm supporting the five tones.*

After completing the instrumental introduction, Bai Niu begins to sing. Her voice is likened to precious gems and her vocal skills are described as nothing short of perfection.

> *While the delicate sounds of the sanxian's strings seem to curl upward,*
> *Bai Niu raises her eyebrows, focuses her gaze, and opens her vermillion lips.*
> *Singing each phrase is like dropping a string of pearls:*
> *Her remarkable voice dazzles the listeners.*
> *And, just as expected, her voice is smooth and polished like a flawless gem*
> *Whose silt and dirt has been washed away.*
> *Her melodies are ingenious*
> *And her lyrics are both simple and yet profound, appealing to everyone;*
> *Her rhythms move freely from fast to slow, as the story demands*
> *And her melodies range from high to low according to her inclination.*

After focusing directly on her vocal abilities, the narrative's descriptions of Bai Niu's voice shift to a synesthetic portrayal of sound using visual metaphors. DeWoskin interprets synesthesia in the Chinese context as a theory of art that "focuses on the commutability of sensations, the exchangeability of objects and images, the intertranslatability of meaning from genre to genre, and, finally the natural interpenetration of art and life" (1982: 172–173). The visual metaphors from the natural world are used to describe the otherworldly sound of the feminine voice in the poem. Dayan explains that one of the values of music stems from its "metaphoricity" (2006: 100). In no place is this more evident than in the commutability of music and the visual metaphors of nature in the story about Bai Niu's voice.

> *When she portrays a solemn scene, it is as though one were looking at a*
>   *desolate, snowy mountain landscape.*
> *Hearing her sing about a pleasant scene is like experiencing the warmth of*
>   *a breezy, verdant spring day.*
> *Listening to her portray a beautiful scene is like witnessing the splendor and*
>   *elegance of Jiangnan.*

> *When singing about an awe-inspiring scene, the listener experiences the*
> *stark magnificence of a desert.*

In some ways, Bai Niu's narrative song is similar to Lakmé's vocal performance at the beginning of Delibes's opera, which begins with Lakmé's
improvisatory, textless vocalizing.[9] Abbate explains that Lakmé's singing
voice compels without the assistance of words because "it is not the story that
acts upon its listener. The act of telling it—the act of narrating—is the point"
(1996: 6). Similarly, the act of Bai Niu telling her story is also the main point
of her performance, especially since the lyrics themselves are never described.
However, unlike those who hear Lakmé's vocalizing, the readers of Zhu's
poem can only vicariously appreciate the effect of Bai Niu's voice on her
listeners through Lao Can's descriptions. While Abbate questions the ability
of literature to adequately evoke music (1996: 18), one might argue that the
poetic description of Bai Niu's voice is the only adequate way to induce her
imaginary performance. Dayan believes that "literature becomes necessary as
soon as music ceases to appear as music ... as soon as we think about it and
lend it meaning" (2006: 94). And so it is with the performance of Bai Niu. The
literary medium is the only way to capture and immortalize the marvels of the
young girl's evanescent voice and its surreal effect on the audience. If it were a
real performance, the ephemerality of music would also arguably necessitate
a literary description to memorialize it, thereby compensating for the transi-
ence of the voice. As a fictive performance of an unheard voice, the necessity
for the literary account becomes even more apparent.

> *Hundreds of listeners in the audience are dumbstruck,*
> *Forgetting to smoke or even pour the water to make tea,*
> *Afraid of disturbing the purity of the sound, no one dares to cheer,*
> *Or otherwise defy the unspoken ban on disturbing the magical ambience.*
> *It is as though Lao Can is drunken as he reverently listens to the*
> *marvelous song,*
> *He is in a trance, not sure where he is, and unable to distinguish true and*
> *false.*
> *All he knows is that the scene in front of him has changed,*
> *The only sound he hears is Bai Niu's song.*

The peculiar capacity of literature to express music is aptly described by
Dayan, who explains a curious contradiction. Music embodies something
beyond words, yet also expresses something that can be translated into words
(2006: 31). He goes on to explain that there is a moment in which music is
perceived as something drawn from the world outside music, followed by
a second moment in which that perception is received as inadequate: "It is
always possible, after that second moment, to reflect back on the first and to
condemn the initial perception, the metaphor, as an illusion; but the illusion
was needed to allow the discourse on music to begin" (2006: 101). Bai Niu's

music is described as being drawn from the natural world, creating a transcendent, hallucinogenic state among members of the audience. Hearing Bai Niu's voice invites the listeners to take a journey to a celestial realm, facilitated by the synesthetic connections between sound and the sights of nature, even though readers of the poem can only vicariously experience the scenes and sounds through words. The illusion is absolutely necessary for the success of the narrative, which works only if readers surrender their imagination to Lao Can's ability to conjure up Bai Niu. As Lao Can reflects on his own altered state while listening to Bai Niu, he provides a compelling narrative about the transcendent power of the female voice.

> *Her voice is like a magnet,*
> *And Lao Can follows after it.*
> *Everywhere he is taken is a place of spectacular beauty, a paradise,*
> *With green mountains and rivers, hidden valleys and secluded woods.*
> *All around him are mountain ridges and peaks, clear and limpid streams,*
> *Verdant cypress and pine trees in a thick carpet of grass.*
> > *Bouquets of flowers, thick bunches of leaves, richly fragrant and abundant,*
> *A hundred birds perching on branches, wasps and butterflies circling around rows of flowers,*
> *A riotous profusion of color.*
> *Then, suddenly, as though it is being pulled from the ground,*
> *Her voice catapults to the highest heavens.*
> *It ascends higher and higher as it soars to breathtaking heights*
> *Before it gradually descends, step by step.*
> *Someone once said, "I doubt I can find my way through the dense mountains and rivers."*
> *It is like finally discovering a village after seeing only tall willows and bright flowers.* [10]
> *Hopefully this song will be preserved for a thousand years,*
> *Enduring for generation after generation in Hushan.*

The story ends when Bai Niu leaves the stage and Lao Can and the other listeners regain consciousness, reluctantly returning to the mundane world. Even then, her voice lingers. DeWoskin explains that non-sounding moments, particularly after musical sounds, are both significant and informed in writings about early Chinese musical aesthetics, and notes that writers in the Chinese musical tradition during the classical period "speak about the 'after-tones' in much the same way that wine-tasters speak about an aftertaste" (1982: 141). Zhu's references to the lingering of Bai Niu's voice, especially in the following stanza, describe the after-tones of her performance and their profound effect on the audience. By invoking early Chinese aesthetics, Zhu likens Bai Niu's voice to ideals that come from the classical past, further emphasizing her elevated status as a being who can communicate supernatural sounds to mortals. Bai Niu, then, is an "audition"—the vocal version of an apparition—whose non-sounding performance is vividly brought to life through literature.

> *Then, suddenly, the clear voice stops,*
> *And Lao Can, as though regaining consciousness after a dream, realizes it*
>   *is over.*
> *Even though Bai Niu has left the stage,*
> *The intoxicating sound remains.*
> *Although the cheers reverberate like thunder,*
> *They cannot compete with the lingering sound of her voice that still*
>   *permeates everywhere.*
> *Lao Can, basking in admiration, remembers the poem, "This song is*
>   *meant for heaven."*
> *"How could earthly beings be so blessed to hear it?"*[11]
> *Those who heard this song on the banks of Daming Lake are fortunate,*
> *Bai Niu's golden voice and peerless performance dazzled countless fans.*

This extraordinary tale about Bai Niu serves as an allegory about, as well as paean to, the significance of the female voice during the early decades of the twentieth century. In this text, the immortalized young woman's bodily appearance is minimized, thereby ameliorating the body problem and making her a prototype for female narrators who sought a vocal career outside of prostitution.[12] The character remains popular eight decades after her description in Liu E's novel, and this figure of a treble voice cloaked in a de-sexualized, metaphysical feminine body has become iconic.

Intelligence in the service of virtue: "Melted Candlesticks"[13]

Although Bai Niu serves as a key example of metaphysical feminine talent, she remains an unusual heroine. Most *quyi* texts exonerate their metaphysical heroines by depicting them as virtuous women confronted with making challenging decisions with deeply moral implications, so their metaphorical "voices" are represented by their intelligence, moral fortitude, and righteousness. The following examples exemplify those figurative—rather than actual—metaphysical feminine voices.

"Melted Candlesticks" (*Hua La Qiar*), an example of the *quyi* genre known as Comic Monologues (*dankou xiangsheng*),[14] features a metaphysical heroine who faces such a challenging decision. In the spirit of Wang Yuejin's description of a femininity complex (1991: 83), the protagonist is an intelligent and virtuous daughter pitted against her greedy and immoral brothers, yet the underlying meaning in this traditionally comical plot is quite serious. As a genre, Comic Monologues focus on the lives of common people, exposing their problems and poking fun at their practices and superstitions, but they are also highly popular among elite audiences (Lawson 2011: 19–20). One of the important messages of this particular story is the emptiness of a social system in which underlings display a feigned respect for authority only for the purpose of self-aggrandizement. The more significant theme in this plot, however, is underestimating of the importance of the woman's role in her natal family.

The story begins as the family is marrying off the daughter, who, according to traditional custom, goes to live with her husband's family. Her three older brothers are already married and living in the natal home. Shortly after her wedding, her father dies, and the three brothers and their wives start bickering about how things should be run in the home. In the end, the brothers decide to distribute the property and go their separate ways. Everything is divided, down to the last copper coin, which buys fried beans that are then divided once again. Their single problem is deciding who will take care of their elderly mother—an issue none of the greedy sons has considered.[15]

Even though the married daughter is theoretically absolved of any filial responsibility toward her mother and is not entitled to an inheritance from her natal family, she is the only child concerned about her mother's welfare. As the brothers continue to argue about how they will take turns caring for her, the mother is neglected and ends up at her daughter's doorstep, sick and emaciated. Since the brothers should have accepted their responsibility to provide for their mother and because the daughter cannot care for her mother without jeopardizing her position in her married family, the daughter devises a plan to ensure that her mother is properly cared for while teaching her brothers a lesson. She melts down the pewter candlesticks that are part of her dowry and molds them into the shapes of gold and silver ingots, then sews these imitation ingots into a pouch that her mother can wear around her waist. The daughter carefully instructs her mother never to let her sons see what is actually in the belt, allowing them to suppose that she is hiding a large sum of money that they will be able to claim after she dies.

Just as the daughter predicts, the three brothers fall for her trick and try their best to outdo one another in order to keep the mother (and the assumed inheritance) in their home with them. Since the mother is finally well fed and is forced to exercise by carrying around the melted candlesticks, her health actually improves, and she lives longer than anyone had expected. When the old woman is finally ready to die, the brothers begin fighting over where she should be when she actually passes away. Each brother tries to prove the superiority of his loyalty by attempting to provide the best possible funeral. None of them sheds a tear for their mother, however, until they discover that the "ingots" are actually melted pewter candlesticks.

Considering the way women have been viewed traditionally in China, "Melted Candlesticks" is an especially interesting piece. Wolf explains:

> The birth of a daughter in traditional China was a disappointment ... They [the daughters] could contribute little or nothing to their natal families in the way of enhancing their status, increasing their wealth, or providing for their care in their old age ... And when the time came for

a girl to be sent off to another family in marriage, most of the bride price had to be spent on her dowry if the family was not to lose its standing within the community. Unfortunately, the cultural stereotypes about the nature of women did nothing to make up for their structural handicaps. Women were narrow-hearted. They were incapable of understanding the finer points of human relations on which all civilized life depended. They gossiped and were jealous and quarrelsome, scolding other members of the family and even the neighbors when aroused. They were ignorant and stupid and irresponsible.

(1985: 1–2)

After reading "Melted Candlesticks," however, the reader understands a very different, even diametrically opposed view of a daughter. While there are many different kinds of Chinese women described in various literary, historical, and anthropological accounts (see Barlow 1994: 253–90), I am arguing that the sympathetic portrayal of the female protagonist in this story clearly illustrates an important contrast between a filial metaphysical heroine and Wolf's reporting of a very different conception about Chinese women. In "Melted Candlesticks," the metaphysical daughter is the only intelligent and moral character, shrewdly outwitting her brothers to provide her victimized mother the care she deserves.

The marked difference between certain cultural stereotypes and the metaphysical heroine of "Melted Candlesticks" may also be explained using Nettl's idea about redistributing energy discussed in Chapter 1 (1985).[16] The shift from a daughter who is removed from her natal family toward this metaphysical daughter is a compensatory gesture that exalts an androgenized femininity by combining the elite feminine characteristics of virtue with the elite masculine characteristics of tactical intelligence, creating an exemplary protagonist who occupies a metaphysical feminine space between conventional masculinity and femininity.

Righteous indignation: "The Courtesan's Jewelbox"[17]

Chinese literary authorship holds a semi-sacred place in Chinese culture, and it is significant that male writers created most of the iconic metaphysical heroines in tragic literary pieces. The logographic script represents historicity, cultural authority, and visual beauty; and serves as the linguistic fountainhead for the huge variety of spoken and written Chinese languages throughout history. The art of writing is highly valued, and literary composition has been exalted throughout Chinese history, thereby endowing metaphysical heroines in written *quyi* narratives with added legitimacy.[18] Furthermore, the advent of printing during the Ming period (1368–1644) led to a publishing boom that allowed more people to read. Texts that were originally written or inspired by Chinese literati of the late Ming and Manchu bannermen (the military elite) of the late Qing were eventually reworked by the early male performers of

Tianjin *quyi*. Although female performers in Republican Tianjin eventually adopted the following texts, it is important to appreciate their origins as literary pieces written by male authors about doomed women.

To fully grasp the role of the intelligent, virtuous, and frequently wronged female protagonists in *quyi* texts, it is essential to consider the historical role of the courtesan—a woman whose preference for literary pursuits and "pure singing" was described in Chapter 1. One of the most important antecedents for narrative literature featuring metaphysical heroines is late sixteenth- and early seventeenth-century courtesan culture, in which poetry-writing male literati formed close connections with courtesan singers who rendered their poetry to music. The tonal nature of the Chinese language has resulted in an unusually close connection between poetry and song, and the resulting creative exchange between male author and female singer was highly significant (Zeitlin 2006: 75).[19] While courtesans in China, like Venetian courtesans of the seventeenth century, were expected to provide sexual and entertainment services (Heller 2003: 17), they also became icons whose archetypical influence continued from the late sixteenth century through the beginning of the twentieth century. Ropp explains that Chinese courtesans were honorary literati, occupying

> the only place in culture where women could openly socialize with men who were not their husbands. The most prominent among them enjoyed a level of renown unattainable by any other type of woman ... [and they often became] powerful symbols of morality and virtue.
>
> (1997: 18)

Li Wai-Yee writes about how the Chinese literati used the image of the courtesan—the talented woman victimized by her social station—to symbolize their own political instability, by emphasizing how courtesans with uncertain social status became icons of refinement and freedom (1997: 46–47). Misfortune was key to the power of the courtesan, and the romanticized image of a tragic courtesan was related to the perception of personal and historical crisis in the minds of the poets who wrote about them.[20]

Male authors used metaphysical feminine figures as mythical archetypes who represented the glory of Chinese culture in a variety of literary and performance genres, but Wang Yuejin argues that powerful female icons in traditional texts neither exonerated nor ameliorated the statuses of actual women (1991: 83). Even though courtesan culture in the seventeenth century was the one place where real women could sing texts featuring metaphysical characters, and their life experiences could contribute to the metaphysical feminine lore, courtesans were tainted by the profession that helped fashion the simulacrum. Consequently, while some courtesans were considered unofficial literati and others were able to marry, many courtesans were unable to improve their social standing or otherwise benefit by singing about metaphysical feminine icons—the very images that provided a powerful cathartic outlet for male writers—because courtesans were, to build upon Dudden's idea, present *in body*. As Wang Yuejin explains, male authors usurped female archetypes and "pushed aside, marginalized, expelled, suspended, bracketed, and exiled [women] into the realm of the imaginary to become icons and absences" (1991: 83–84). Metaphysical femininity was a site of expression only for disenfranchised male writers and performers.[21]

One of the most beloved examples of metaphysical femininity in the repertoire of Tambourine Drumsong (*danxiar*), a popular *quyi* genre that was originally part of a male storytelling tradition, is a piece entitled "The Courtesan's Jewel Box" (*Du Shiniang*), a traditional sixteenth-century tale about courtesan named Decima (the tenth girl in her quarter).[22] Decima saves enough money to buy her freedom and return with her lover Li Jia to his home in Zhejiang province, where he has promised to marry her. Li betrays her, however, when he tries to sell her to Sun Fu, another man who has offered a substantial sum of money for her. Deeply hurt by this betrayal, Decima commits suicide. Before she dies, she shows Li a box containing jewels that are worth many times the amount of money Sun had offered. She had intended to use the money to help him become established and to win over the hearts of his parents, but she takes it with her to her watery grave in defiance of his betrayal.[23] The lowly courtesan is eulogized as a heroine because of the purity of her love for a man who was not worthy of her. The following excerpt of the last few lines, translated by Pian, demonstrates Decima's righteous indignation.

> *How I have been wronged! Yet my wrath will sink with me,*
> *For this ill-fated maid will die today.*
> *She weeps and weeps, with her face in her hands;*
> *And now she twists her eyebrows, closes her eyes, clenches her teeth,*
>   *braces her heart;*
> *With a stamp of her foot, she jumps off the boat.*
> *The frightened, guilty Sun Fu, he is out of his wits;*
> *And that mercenary, cruel, brutal, callous Li Jia shakes with his knees,*
>   *buckling under him.*
> *And so this is my story of Decima, who had met the wrong man;*
> *She cast her treasures in the river and then threw herself in.*
> *It is a legend that everyone sings about, sighs about.*
> *Such is Decima, she was strong and heroic, but she met a hard fate*
>
>   (Pian 2011: 325).

While her employment as a courtesan may have defiled her outwardly, Decima's inner self is above reproach, and her ability to save her resources to support her lover demonstrates her business savvy. The emphasis on the moral courage and intelligence of the betrayed female victim is the essence of the intelligent, righteous martyr, making Decima a powerful metaphysical heroine. As mentioned in Chapter 1, Shi Huiru eventually appropriated this piece from her male competitors and made it her signature work. The combination of Decima's virtue and Shi's homely physical appearance directed attention away from Shi's body and allowed audiences to focus on the righteousness of the character and the beauty of Shi's voice, making Shi's performances of "The Courtesan's Jewelbox" an aesthetic and emotional tour-de-force.

Honorable self-sacrifice: "The Slopes of *Changban*"[24]

In addition to the Chinese literati, Manchu bannermen, the privileged military class of the Qing dynasty, used similar images of wronged women in a performed genre that served as the literary predecessor of some of the important narrative genres that became popular in Tianjin. The Manchu *zidishu*[25] was a narrative art form that flourished from the end of the seventeenth century through the middle of the nineteenth century in Beijing, with its last performances occurring several decades before urban Chinese *quyi* became popular and widespread in Tianjin. A small but significant portion of the *zidishu* repertoire typically featured unusually tragic female figures. As Mary Scott explains, the emergent *zidishu* became an important outlet for the ruling Manchu elite, which was an increasingly disenfranchised group during the latter part of the Qing dynasty (1991: 1). As the power of the Manchus receded, the bannermen began singing about victimized Chinese women as symbols of their plight, because images of women were among the most vivid representations of the wealth and sophistication of the conquered nation (Scott 1991: 9–10). In an ironic historical twist, Manchu leaders sang songs about wronged women just as their Chinese predecessors had done at the end of the Ming dynasty, when the Chinese faced the impending Manchu rule.

After the fall of the Qing dynasty, Chinese male authors and performers continued to employ tragic heroines in their stories. Several decades after the last of the emotionally gripping performances of the Manchu *zidishu*, Chinese peasant singers of narrative tales (all of whom were male) consulted and adapted *zidishu* texts that provided beautifully written lyrics about tragic women for subsequent generations of Chinese narrative performers. Tianjin *quyi* was originally performed by Chinese men who preferred to sing stories about heroines, often using Manchu *zidishu* texts. For example, Liu Baoquan, the legendary male singer of Beijing Drumsong, consulted the *zidishu* version of a piece known as "The Slopes of Changban" (*Changbanpo*), which was written by Han Xiaochuang, a Manchu author who "made something of a specialty of writing pieces which describe the travails of women" (Stevens 1975: 180). Liu Baoquan set Han's lyrics to the Beijing opera-influenced musical style he had developed. While Liu's repertoire consisted of some 25 pieces, his masterpiece was the *zidishu*-derived "The Slopes of Changban," which glorified the female protagonist (Stevens 1990: 90).

Based on an episode from Luo Guanzhong's well-known novel *Romance of the Three Kingdoms* (*Sanguo Yanyi*), Liu Baoquan's "The Slopes of Changban" focuses on the plight of the severely wounded Lady Mi, second wife of one of the rulers of the warring kingdoms. After a battle, the lady and her lord's only heir, the infant A Dou, have been separated from their people. Because she senses the defeat of her husband's army, Lady Mi feels that she must preserve her honor by committing suicide. If she does, however, the young prince will die, so she resolves to live and raise the child. At this point, General Zhao appears on the scene and tries to persuade her to ride away to safety on his horse. She explains that she is in no condition to ride back to camp and tries to convince Zhao that he must instead save the infant. Zhao refuses to leave her, so Lady Mi devises a way to ensure that the child will be taken to safety. Stevens translates the last section as follows:

> *General Zhao, keep this in your heart; now take the child and go.*
> *But Zhao would not take the princeling, urged Lady Mi to mount.*
> *The lady said, "See over there, the enemy forces come."*
> *Zhao Yun turned back, to get a clear look.*
> *That wise and determined woman*
> *Took the weeping infant, resolutely set him down;*
> *She spun about and cast herself into the well, her spirit sent to the shades.*
> *Gladly she chose the right, found eternal rest;*
> > *Bury the moth eyebrows in the rush of the Lo River, the chill of the*
> > *west wind.*
> *Her praise shall be*
> *Pure as gold or jade, word and deed equally fine,*
> *His heroism*
> *A red sun in clear sky, "loyal and just" made plain.*
> *Zhao Zilong's spear*
> *Pushed over the earthen wall, covered the well mouth over;*
> *As he girded for*
> *A break through enemy lines to save A Dou and go to meet Liu Bei.*
> (Stevens 2011: 411–412)

One of the most important messages of the story is that Lady Mi, who was supremely virtuous in her decision to become a martyr, knowingly sacrificed herself for the child and her lord's kingdom. Stevens mentions that other narrative genres that tell this story are often more interested in Zhao's plight than in Lady Mi's sacrifice, so it is significant that Han's version of the text is written with such overwhelming sympathy for Lady Mi (Stevens 1975: 195).

The practice of featuring heroines continued in Liu Baoquan's *quyi* genre known as Beijing Drumsong, as Han's version was the one adopted by Liu in creating his narrative masterwork and also by Liu's growing number of female students.[26] Capitalizing on the trend to highlight a feminine point of view, female narrators were in an optimal position to appropriate these stories and transfer the cultural power of metaphysical heroines to themselves. The following example is an especially powerful case in point.

Tragic ill treatment: "Listening to the Bells at Sword Pavilion"[27]

"Listening to the Bells at Sword Pavilion" (*Jiangewenling*), another example of a *zidishu*-inspired poem, is one of the greatest pieces in the Beijing
Drumsong repertoire and a key example of female narrators appropriating
metaphysical feminine texts. A relatively short literary piece, "Listening"
consists of 38 couplets, compared to the more than 140 couplets of some
drumsong pieces. The basic story is well known to all Chinese: Emperor
Tang Minghuang succumbs to pressure to execute Yang Guifei, his beloved
concubine, in order to salvage his weakening political position. Manchu
author Han Xiaochuang, who also wrote the original text on which "The
Slopes of Changban" is based, implies that Lady Yang became a scapegoat
for the ills of the emperor's reign, and that the entire piece is an expression
of the emperor's remorse for choosing to maintain his political control rather
than save the woman he loved.[28] While Lady Yang is the heroine of the tale,
her voice is never heard in the poem, which focuses solely on the emperor's
expression of grief. Nonetheless, her absence through death intensifies her
power over the emperor. As a heroine who inhabits the space between life
and death,[29] Lady Yang is a ghostly example of a metaphysical heroine whose
lingering power over the emperor is not unlike the after-tones of Bai Niu's
song. Racked by guilt because of his abandonment of her, he is left only with
tormented memories, or "after-experiences."

In the same way that "Bai Niu Tells a Story" (and much of the rest of Chinese
narrative literature) is adapted from other artistic works, so "Listening"
comes from a long line of literary predecessors. Regarding the practice of
adaptation, Linda Hutcheon explains:

> Adaptation is how stories evolve and mutate to fit new times and dif-
> ferent places. Dawkins' postulating of the existence of those units of
> imitation or cultural transmission he calls "memes" seems to me to be
> potentially very productive. Memes are not high-fidelity replicators: they
> change with time, for meme transmission is subject to constant mutation.
> Stories too propagate themselves when they catch on; adaptations—as
> both repetition and variation—are their form of replication. Evolving by
> cultural selection, traveling stories adapt to local cultures, just as popula-
> tions of organisms adapt to local environments.
>
> (2013: 176–177)

For Chinese writers, artists, and musicians, however, expounding on existing
cultural memes is not simply a form of replication; it constitutes the very
meaning of art. William T. de Bary's notion of a "burden of culture" suggests
that Chinese creators (and the Manchu authors who adopted Chinese literary
genres) have a responsibility to work with existing cultural tropes, ideas, and
stories across all media and genres (2001: 573). Creativity and originality are
evaluated in terms of how well artists stay true to the spirit of the meme while

adding a new feature or element. One could argue that adaptation in China is the conscious, reverential replication of existing cultural memes with the thought of humbly offering a contribution to the lore.

As an example of such an adaptation, the 38 couplets of "Listening to the Bells at Sword Pavilion" are based loosely on chapter 29 of a 50-act play entitled *The Palace of Everlasting Life* (*Changshengdian*), written by Hong Sheng in 1688 (Zeitlin 2007: 181). This play was, in turn, deeply influenced by an early poem written by Tang-dynasty poet Bai Juyi, entitled, "Song of Everlasting Sorrow" (*Chang Hen Ge*), and a play written by Yuan dynasty writer Bai Pu, entitled *Pawlonia Tree Rain* (*Wutong Yu*). Based on the tragic love between Emperor Tang Minghuang and his beloved Lady Yang Guifei, this narrative meme has held cultural currency for well over a millennium. The historical event on which the story is based is Lady Yang's death after the infamous An Lushan rebellion in 755. While fleeing the capital in 756, the emperor's troops rebelled at the Mawei Courier Station. After murdering her cousin Yang Guozhong, the rebels forced the emperor to agree to Lady Yang's execution. Although the rebellion was quelled, the emperor's son assumed the throne and the emperor lived the rest of his life in mourning. In Hong Sheng's version, *The Palace of Everlasting Life*, Lady Yang dies by suicide rather than by execution. The first part of the play details her death and the second part recalls the past as the emperor mourns her passing until the two lovers are eventually reunited as immortals (Zeitlin 2007: 182–188).

Hong Sheng's theatrical adaptation of the story uses Lady Yang, the metaphysical heroine, to epitomize the Chinese nostalgia felt for the loss of the Ming dynasty during the early years of Manchu rule in the Qing dynasty. As Zeitlin explains, the death of a palace lady "stands in metonymic relationship to the demise of the entire dynasty" (2007: 104). "Listening," however, presents the story with a twist, as it is written from the vantage point of Han, a member of the Manchu elite in the waning years of the Qing. In "Listening" we hear only the emperor's sadness and hopelessness through his narrative lament; there is no hint of reunification for the two lovers. A deceased woman might appear as a ghost in some texts (Zeitlin 2007: 10–11), so the absence of any ghostly appearance in this version is notable. The only possible reference to Lady Yang is the literary reference to the sound of the bells in the eaves of the Sword Pavilion, where the emperor spends a sleepless night. I surmise that Han—as a Manchu who represented an increasingly disenfranchised population in the latter part of the Qing—identified himself and his people with the wronged Lady Yang in the same way Hong Sheng may have done under radically different historical circumstances. Han's portrayal of the defeated, hopeless emperor may well have symbolized the impotent Chinese nation for the Manchu bannermen. In other words, by choosing this ending in his adaptation of the story, Han is communicating a political message about his people through a deceased metaphysical heroine and her powerless, ineffectual husband. No matter the political interpretation of Lady Yang, her role as a metaphysical heroine works equally well for a wronged Chinese or Manchu author. In both cases, the emphasis on the tragic female victim is in keeping with the argument that metaphysical feminine figures symbolized marginalized males who sensed their fragile and unstable position.

"Listening" is divided into five sections.[30] Section 1 is a brief summary of the events surrounding the emperor's visit to Sword Pavilion at Mawei Courier Station, where Yang hanged herself from a pear tree. It begins by referring to a *tibishi*, a poem, inscribed on a cliff, that testifies to the absence of Lady Yang (Zeitlin 2007: 65). "Listening" is considered a *huaigu*—a poetic reflection stimulated by a visit to a burial site, and its author instills in readers an impulse to recall her life and the wrongs committed against her without ever having to visit the site (89). The following is my translation in italics, interspersed with commentary.

> *On the hillside of Mawei, where the grass is lush and green,*
> *The tomb of the concubine remains to this day.*
> *Inscribed on the cliff is a poem about deep, gnawing regret,*
> *And visiting the memorial shrine, one cannot avoid being sickened by grief.*
> *After embarking on the long trek westward of 10,000 miles,*
> *Why must the emperor endure the sounds of bells and the sighs of a rainy*
>   *night?*
> *Yang Guifei's fragrant soul has fled the pear tree.*[31]
> *Leading the troops, General Chen Yuanli*[32] *escorts the imperial carriage*
>   *on its journey.*

The emperor is deeply despondent. Startled by sounds outside his bedchamber, the emperor learns that they are only the sounds of the bells in the eaves as they mingle with the rain. Having hoped that the sounds meant his beloved had finally returned from the grave, he now becomes even more inconsolable. Even when he speaks about the pear tree as the site of her death, the sound of the word for "pear" (*li*) is homophonous with the word "to depart."

Zeitlin remarks that sounds, as well as apparitions, represent ghosts in Chinese ghost lore. She explains,

> The acoustic manifestation of a phantom, often in disembodied form, is of equal importance [to the visual] in the Chinese literary imagination. No Chinese term for ghost involves sight per se. In contrast, the three most common English terms all have Latin or Greek root meanings pertaining to vision: "specter" (to look, to see); "apparition" (to appear): "phantom" (present to the eye). A preoccupation with a ghost's *optical* dimension is deeply embedded in English and the Romance languages, but this one-sidedness may be a peculiarly European phenomenon, enhanced in recent years with the critical turn toward visuality and visual culture
>
> (2007: 53–4).

Lady Yang's auditory presence may well be the sound of bells in the eaves of the pavilion where the emperor is staying, and is contrasted with the sound of the rain, which corresponds metonymically to the tears of the emperor. The combination of rain and bells is particularly disquieting for the emperor, as it seems to be mocking his grief.

> *The emperor sighs amidst feelings of pervasive despair and persistent*
>   *loneliness,*
> *Drunken with sorrow, his tears flow.*
> *Acknowledging the desolation of the dim light of the crescent moon and the*
>   *stars just before dawn,*
> *He wonders how he can bear the remote journey, with rivers to traverse and*
>   *mountains to climb.*
> *With great difficulty he tries to imagine the palace where he can rest his*
>   *weary body,*
> *But encountering cold rain and icy wind only intensifies his misery.*
> *In the Sword Pavilion the Son of Heaven cannot sleep,*
> *Outside the window he hears the incessant patter of raindrops.*
> *Hurriedly he asks, "What is the sound outside the window?"*
> *Gao Lishi*[33] *reports, "The forest raindrops mingle with the sounds of the*
>   *bells under the eaves."*
> *When the emperor hears this, he sighs deeply,*
> *He replies "A broken-hearted man hears heart-rending sounds."*

The emperor's despondence increases with the unrelenting sounds of the bells and the rain, intensified by the cold and the dim light of a single lamp in the pavilion. Remembering the goddess of Wu Mountain, he compares himself to the ancient King of Chu who was reputed to have met the goddess in a dream. The story is often used metaphorically to describe the thwarted love between a man and a woman, and the emperor's story similarly ends unhappily. The emperor also recalls a legend about another fabled beauty, the goddess of the Luo River, who refuses to leave the river to meet her lover, and the emperor fears that Lady Yang will similarly ignore his entreaties. Halfway through the section, Han uses a literary technique known as "piled-up phrases" (*duo ju*) to pose a series of hypothetical questions as to why she has not come back to see him: Could it be …?. The emperor eventually suggests his own answer.

> *In the end, it is the troubling sound of bells merging with the disquieting*
>   *sound of rain,*
> *"How can I sever the thoughts and stop the feelings?"*
> *The persistent tapping of raindrops on the window, knocking on the door of*
>   *my breaking heart,*
> *The relentless sounds of rattling branches keep me from dreaming.*
> *Dang lang lang—the frightening sounds from the eaves approach in front,*

As the bone-rattling cold rises from the depths of the quilt.
The light from a solitary lamp creates a single shadow,
"With whom can I speak during the fifth watch of this rainy night?
In ancient times the goddess of Wu Mountain entered the dreams of the
    King of Chu,
How is it that when I want to dream of you, I cannot?
Could it be that your delicate feet[34] are too lazy to step out into the
    moonlight[35]?
Could it be that the sleeve of your garment does not protect you against the
    midnight breeze?
Could it be that you are bored by the weary travelers at the inn?
Could it be that the sounds of the soldiers' galloping horses frighten you?
Could it be that you, my beautiful wife, still harbor bitterness?
Could it be that you think my unfaithful heart lacks sincerity?
Since the goddess will not leave Luopu,
I am left to wait upon your spirit while my tears run dry."

The emperor comes close to admitting his guilt in the next section. He invokes the story of Chang E, who allegedly trained Lady Yang in the rainbow dance, and wonders why Lady Yang engaged in a journey she could not finish. Like Chang E, who only made it to the moon, which is considered halfway to heaven, Lady Yang appears to be either unable or, worse, unwilling to complete the journey back to him. As he rehearses the events on the day she died, he regrets his decision to give so much military power to An Lushan and bemoans the hatred that was directed at her. He recognizes that she died to save him, yet he stops short of accepting full responsibility for mismanaging the affairs of the country. His impotence as a leader and a husband makes him a compelling character for a Manchu writer looking to place political blame.

"One of us is alone in the bedchamber, the pillow and quilt are icy cold,
The other, a true beauty, is buried in a tomb of yellow earth.
Two trees that once grew together are blown apart by a violent rainstorm,
    one to the left and one to the right,
Two lovebirds who once shared wings[36] are blown apart by a fierce wind,
    sending one to the east and one to the west.
In this life there is no hope for the perfect pair to be together,
I can only hope to follow you on the path to the afterlife.
I imagine that you will naturally return to your palace on the moon like
    Chang E,[37]
But why did you leave when, like her, you would only make it half way to
    the immortal world?
I regret that so much military power was mistakenly given to your
    cousin,[38]
And wish that the national affairs had been entrusted to someone else.

As I consider what happened, traitors harmed the country,
Unjustly maligning you as a femme fatale.
Filled with bitterness and hatred, military generals opposed you,
Ashamed, I wanted to protect your remaining years, yet could not.
Your pitiable spirit, like a thread dispersed by the wind,
Causes my tears of blood to flow like rain.
Facing deadly peril, your eyes were wide open, your white teeth chattered
*   with fear,*
Your precious body shivered, and your facial expression was tragic.
Looking helplessly at you, I could not save you nor take your place,
Deeply grieved, how can I redress the injustice or even face you?
Profoundly broken hearted, once a year I visit when the pear blossoms fall,
Sorrowing whenever I see a pear tree.
My wife, ah, you were maligned in order to protect me,
At present, struggling with feelings of remorse, I also recall the tender
*   feelings of our past together."*

In the final section, the emperor recounts all the activities that the couple will
no longer do together. The sounds of the bells have become more sporadic, as
though she is signalling her disinterest; at the same time, the rain has intensified, representing the emperor's tears and unrelenting grief. The poem ends
when the emperor begins the rest of the journey after a miserable, sleepless
night.

"We can no longer gaze at the dual blossomed lotus[39] in the Taiye Pond,
Nor pen verse and tunes at the Chenxiang Pavilion.
We can no longer enjoy looking at the moon, tête-à-tête, at the Wanyue
*   Tower,*
Nor wish each other the blessings of immortality in the Pavilion of Eternal
*   Life.*
As we whispered our passionate thoughts to each other late into the night,
You responded that a loving couple would be together forever.
Until now your words still ring in my ears, but where are you?
All I am left with are many thoughts and feelings of pain and remorse.
Outside the window the sounds of the bells are now sporadic, yet the rain
*   intensifies,*
Within my chamber the remaining light from the lamp barely lingers, the
*   imperial bed is like ice.*
My stomach is deeply tied in knots and wants to burst,
My teardrops, colored with blood, flow profusely."
Grief stricken, the emperor goes without sleep the entire night until dawn,
When his trusted eunuch requests that they continue with their journey.

This poem is one of the greatest literary masterworks in all of Tianjin *quyi*
and worked as an excellent source text for the women of *quyi*. While female

narrators were probably not aware of the historical practice of using female protagonists by Chinese or Manchu male authors, an elegantly written story about a metaphysical feminine character like Lady Yang would undoubtedly have been attractive to female singers. In particular, the tragic story about Lady Yang must have been especially appealing to Luo Yusheng, who made this piece her masterwork. The absence of the heroine was significant for Luo, as though the text were an invitation for her to become the auditory presence of Lady Yang—an example of music completing what the literary piece began. As Dayan clarifies, literature "only becomes art when we read it as performing something that goes beyond understanding and therefore beyond its own primary function" (2006: 87–88). This explains the unusual transformation that takes place when the lyrics of "Listening" become fully realized through music. In setting the lyrics to music, Luo, the storyteller, explores the boundaries between music and language, perfecting both the literary and the musical in the process. As a musically rendered poem, the sound of performance not only conjures up the world of audibility, which Zeitlin argues is the world of the supernatural (2007: 54–56), but, according to early Chinese cosmology, the lingering after-tones have the capability of penetrating our minds even more deeply than by sound alone.

The texts referred to in this chapter exemplify the talent, intelligence, righteous indignation, self-sacrifice, and tragic ill treatment associated with metaphysical heroines, who provided a potent cathartic outlet for the male authors who originally conceived them and an ennobling performance opportunity for the male performers who portrayed them. Once women were given the chance to ascend public stages as reputable performers in the early years of the twentieth century, female narrators appropriated these same texts, using their own powerful feminine voices to bring their heroines to life. In so doing, the women of *quyi* realized the poetry through their singing voices and became the musical successors to the male authors and performers who created metaphysical femininity.

Notes

1 While female impersonation was the ideal in public theatrical performance, refer to the second half of Chapter 1 for some examples of female performers.

2 Some of the material contained in this chapter and in Chapter 1 appeared previously in Lawson (2014a). This material is included with permission from the editor of *Modern Chinese Literature and Culture*.

3 See note 5 for more information about the circumstances behind this piece.

4 It is noteworthy that the audience is composed of men, since women did not attend public performances until the late 1920s (Goldstein 2007: 69). However, as I will argue, Bai Niu was not viewed sexually in the novel or in this piece, so the draw for these male attendees was her voice. She was able to direct attention towards her celestial vocal abilities and away from her body because of her status as an androgynous metaphysical heroine.

5 Ironically, even though the poem was actually set to music shortly after it was

written, the musical setting was not nearly as well received as the poem itself. Zhu won first place for the poem in a national competition, whereas the singer was only awarded second place for her performance. While many believe there were political reasons why the singer did not receive first place, the singer herself acknowledges that the narrative is extremely difficult to perform. How can a mortal sing a story whose purpose is to describe an immortal voice? Because of the challenges in rendering the voice of Bai Niu, this particular narrative piece about the illusory voice of a fictive female storyteller is not performed as often as other standard pieces in this narrative genre, and one might argue that it is better appreciated through reading. Conversely, in Chapter 3, I discuss another example that proves the opposite—a piece in which the narrative is better appreciated through the act of listening than through reading, demonstrating a different kind of liminality between words and music.

6 The complete Chinese text for Zhu's poem is found in appendix 1.

7 The *sanxian*, drum, and clappers mentioned in the poem are commonly used instruments in the narrative arts. The *sanxian* is a three-stringed, long-necked plucked lute. It is considered the primary accompanying instrument in a *quyi* ensemble. For introductory information about the structure and playing techniques of the *sanxian*, see Stevens (1975: 143–144). For information about the drum and clappers, see Stevens (1975: 137–142) and Lawson (2011: 77–78).

8 See Brindley (2012:64–82) about the integral relationship between sound and the cosmos in early Chinese history.

9 While Abbate's arguments concern the relationship between text and tune in a very different musical genre than Chinese *quyi*, there is one major similarity in these two instances. In both Delibes's opera and in "Bai Niu Tells a Story" the textless vocalizations are significant. Suffice it to say that it is the very act of singing in both examples that makes them comparable.

10 This is a reference to a poem by the Song-dynasty poet Lu You (Yu), in which he describes a densely wooded area. See Lu (1973: 3) for a translation of the entire poem.

11 Using this line from Du Fu's (Tu Fu) poem about heavenly music, Zhu emphasizes the otherworldly nature of this performance. See Hung (1952: 179) for a translation of the entire poem.

12 Although acting was also increasingly available as a career option for women in twentieth-century Tianjin, there were serious social problems associated with the acting profession, as mentioned in Chapter 1.

13 I was given an out-of-print version of this text by Professor Xue Baokun after an interview with him in 1985 (1985a). According to Xue, this was a popular story in Tianjin during the early decades of the twentieth century. I have since been unable to locate a published version of the work, but I provide a complete transcription of the original text I received in Appendix 2.

14 See Tsau (1979–80) and Link (1980, 1984, 1986) for an explanation of Comic Routines (*xiangsheng*) in English. Information specifically about Comic Monologues (*dankou xiangsheng*) is found in Zhang (1983: 5–8). For a discussion of the importance of the satirical messages of Comic Routines, see Lawson (2011: 122–124).

15 In the Confucian tradition, taking care of his aging parents is the single most important obligation for a son. The fact that none of the three sons is concerned about their mother is shocking.

16 As discussed in Chapter 1, I am extending the logic he uses in discussing redistributing musical energy to redistributing gender energy.

17 I am using Pian's 2011 translation of this text, based on a recording by Shi Huiru from 1962. See Pian (1979) for a musical transcription of this piece.

18 See Lawson (2011: 82–84) for a discussion about how *quyi* texts are composed.
19 The language used for the majority of Tianjin *quyi* genres is standard Mandarin or *putonghua*, which employs four tones for stressed syllables. See Lawson (2011: 131–132) for an explanation of speech tones in Mandarin; (2011: 47–56) for a discussion of the relationship between language and music; and (2011: 59–95) for examples of the way melody interacts with speech tone in specific genres.
20 For more information about these female characters, see Rebollo-Sborgi (2001: 258–265).
21 The women of *quyi* were eventually able to appropriate metaphysical femininity because they de-emphasized their female sexuality as third-person narrators and, therefore, cleverly circumnavigated the body problem.
22 I allude to this story twice in Chapter 1—once in the context of prostitute singers and again in reference to Shi Huiru, a famous female narrator from Tianjin. "Decima" is Pian's translation of the heroine's name (1979, 2011).
23 See Pian for two versions of her translation for this story (1979, 2011).
24 This text is taken from a recent translation by Catherine Stevens (2011: 406–412). An earlier translation, accompanied by more discussion about the work, is found in Stevens (1990).
25 For a good compilation of important *zidishu* texts, refer to Zhongguo Quyixie Liaoningfenhui (1979). For an excellent introduction to and discussion of *zidishu*, refer to Cui (2005).
26 Interestingly, Han's positive portrayal of Lady Mi over General Zhao is not unlike the way Mei Lanfang, the famous male *dan* who was a contemporary of Liu Baoquan, re-created his character of Concubine Yu as the protagonist who overshadows the king in his version of *Farewell My Concubine* (*Bawang Bieji*). Mei acknowledges Liu Baoquan's efforts to upgrade his drumsong genre (quoted in Stevens 1990: 69, n1), and follows suit in the way he reinterpreted Concubine Yu as morally superior to her husband, the king, in his highly popular signature work. As prominent early twentieth-century male performers elevated the statuses of their feminine characters through texts and in performance, they unwittingly prepared the way for female narrators, such as Sun Shujun and Zhang Cuifeng, to adopt reworked stories like "The Slopes of Changban" as their own masterworks.
27 Tianjin *quyi* scholar Wang Xiuxun transcribed the Chinese lyrics (found in Appendix 3) from Luo Yusheng's classic 1961 recording. My translation of the lyrics into English follows later in the chapter.
28 The political implications of this story for a Manchu author are discussed shortly.
29 While Zeitlin's concept of a phantom heroine (2007) appears to be similar to my notion of a metaphysical heroine, they are nonetheless different since metaphysical heroines are not necessarily ghosts. In this case, however, the metaphysical Lady Yang is also a phantom heroine.
30 Stevens provides an excellent introduction to the literary structure of Beijing Drumsong (1975: 104–125).
31 According to the story told in *Changsheng dian*, she was hanged from a pear tree.
32 This is the same general who was responsible for having Yang Guifei and her cousin Yang Guozhong killed in order to stop the An Lushan rebellion.
33 Gao is the emperor's most trusted eunuch.
34 The description of her feet is a reference to her bound feet—a practice whereby the feet of women were bent back to resemble a bow.
35 The reference is to the third watch, which is between 11:00 p.m. and 1:00 a.m.
36 This refers to an image of a pair of lovebirds, each of which has one wing. Together they are whole and can fly.
37 Chang E was reported to have stolen an elixir of immortality from her husband,

whereupon she flew to a palace on the moon. However, since the moon is only halfway to the immortal world, she remained stranded there with only a rabbit for company.

38 This is a reference to Yang Guifei's adopted son, An Lushan, who became an enemy of Yang's cousin, Yang Guozhong. Their animosity was one of the factors that led to An's Rebellion in 755. The emperor fled to Mawei, taking Yang Guifei with him. There, under the direction of General Chen Xuanli (the general commander of the army), Yang Guozhong was killed. General Chen urged the emperor to have Yang Guifei killed because the Yang family had incited the rebellion. Yang Guifei was therefore forced to hang herself to redeem the reputation of the emperor and save the empire from internal strife. The emperor is under General Chen's protection as he makes the current journey.

39 Two blossoms on a stalk is a symbol of a devoted couple.

3 Musical Voices
Balancing Text and Tune

Each defines itself through the other, at the same time as each rejects the other. Music writes literature, and literature writes music; neither can compose itself alone.

Peter Dayan (2006: x)

Western scholars and critics often discuss an inherent antagonism between language and music in Western opera. Poizat explains:

Inevitably, if the work is beautiful and the interpretation good, certain passages will wrest your attention from the printed words: you lean back in your chair and lose yourself in listening, oblivious for all the world to the printed text. It is then that the libretto drops out of your hands. The attitude is in conflict with your original project of listening attentively to the verbal exchange, as it is precisely at these powerful moments, when the singer's expressive qualities and the meaning of the words ought to come together in the deepest sense, that you should be most attentive to the literary text. Yet somehow you feel a radical antagonism between letting yourself be swept away by the emotion and applying yourself to the meaning of each word as it is sung. You must choose; and if for example the demands of scholarship make it essential that you follow the text word for word, you can do so only at great expense in terms of concentrated effort and lost *jouissance*.

(1991: 199)

Koestenbaum raises the same issue about the rivalry between language and music in his discussion about Strauss's last opera, *Capriccio*, which poses the same question that "inspired the invention of opera: which is primary, words or music?" (2001: 193), as though the listener must declare allegiance to one or the other.

No such antagonism fuels the relationship between libretto and melody in the Chinese narrative arts. The stories sung by the women of *quyi* operate very differently, displaying a fluid, evenly balanced interplay between language and music. The symbiosis of lyrics and vocal sonority—what Barthes would call the pheno-song and geno-song, respectively (1977: 181–183)—constitutes the hallmark achievement of Chinese female narrators. The women of *quyi* achieved an artistic balance between text and tune by introducing a new level of musical skill that surpassed the abilities of their male progenitors and competitors while simultaneously communicating their lyrics with the greatest literary and linguistic care. The music created by the women of *quyi* matched the literary qualities of these texts, and created an aesthetic balance that exceeded the artistry of previous generations of male narrators.

In order to appreciate this achievement, it is important to understand the significance of both the literary and musical components of narrative performance. As mentioned in the previous chapter, the written word is revered because it bears the imprimatur of Chinese culture. Writing embodies all the richness of language, history, and art in its script, and literate Chinese have traditionally delighted in the linguistic beauty of a beloved story, written in elegant language. At the same time, educated Chinese audiences have expected an equally high level of artistry in the vocal rendition of words, and unlettered audiences have depended on sung narratives for their cultural edification and entertainment, as well as their aesthetic pleasure. Further complicating the relationship between text and tune, the linguistic tones of the Chinese language limit how words and music can match up, and challenge the singers to make these matches more than just linguistically functional.[1] Chinese listeners from all walks of life relish hearing the way music fulfills the lyrics by realizing linguistic word tone through vocal artistry, simultaneously pushing the boundaries of semantic meaning and unleashing musical beauty. Rendering the text through song has traditionally represented the most complete version of a Chinese story—a perfect synesthetic exchange between the arts of literature and music. The women of *quyi* became great exemplars of narrative performance because of their ability to endow the musical side of performance with a new level of sophistication while still communicating and enhancing the literary beauty of the lyrics.

A female singing style

When female narrators in Tianjin first captivated audiences with their distinctly feminine voices and de-emphasized bodies, they created a vocal sensation comparable to the literary impression made by Bai Niu. As female singers gradually monopolized the performance of sung genres in the narrative arts, singing eventually became viewed as a quintessentially feminine form of expression in Tianjin *quyi* (Wang, Yubao 1991, Lu 1991), protected by the androgyny of their roles as narrators. Audiences could focus on the femininity of their voices because their bodies were minimized in performance. The Tianjin *quyi* community frequently uses the terms *yinyuehua* ("musicalization") and *nuxinghua* ("feminization") to refer to the musical influence of female narrators that began in the Republican period (Xue 1985a), and nowhere was this influence more evident than in the genre known as Tianjin Popular Tunes. The most musically ornate of the Tianjin genres, the lyrics are fitted to pre-existing melodies; the meter is regular; and the vocal style is highly melismatic,[2] all of which were considered "feminine" characteristics (Wang, Yubao 1991), and as a result, female performers have dominated this genre since the Republican period.

While no other genre is quite as musically ornamented as Tianjin Popular Tunes, many other Tianjin narrative genres that have been appropriated by female singers also display what *quyi* aficionados refer to as a high degree of musicality.[3] Beijing Drumsong, the most respected sung genre in Tianjin, also features different styles of singing that are differentiated by gender. By the 1970s, most of the performers of Beijing Drumsong in the Tianjin Municipal *Quyi* Arts Troupe were divided into the two major schools at the time: the male or Liu style after Liu Baoquan (1869–1942), and the female or Luo style after Luo Yusheng (1914–2002).[4] The gender differences between the two schools notwithstanding, the majority of the performers have been female— even in the male school.[5]

To clarify what constituted the gender distinctions between these two schools of singing, I compare two renditions of "At Break of Day" (since it is one of the few pieces performed by singers in both schools) to ascertain the musical differences that make one "male" and the other "female."[6] The following analysis features second-generation students from each of the two schools. Xiao Lanyun (1923–1992),[7] a highly respected performer who studied with Liu Baoquan when she was a young girl, represents the male style of the Liu school. Lu Yiqin (1933), one of Luo Yusheng's disciples,[8] represents the female style of Luo Yusheng, whose significance as the only school of singing founded by a female is remarkable. Appendix 4 includes a complete transcription of the vocal lines from both renditions, printed line by line to demonstrate the comparison between the two styles of singing.

Differences between male and female styles

Vocal techniques

In all examples of the Beijing Drumsong genre, the first or "top" line (T-1) is a technical showcase for the performer.[9] As far as "At Break of Day" is concerned, this line illustrates most of the major differences between the male and female schools in terms of melody, rhythm, register, and singing style better than any other line in the piece. A comparison of this line performed by the two singers is transcribed as Example 3.1. In the male style, Xiao Lanyun's opening line is longer and more melodically disjunct; emphasizes a higher part of the register; and demonstrates a good deal of parlando, which is a kind of heightened speech of "feminization" in indefinite pitches, each of which is notated with an "x" on the staff. In the female style, Lu's melody is more conjunct; employs more grace notes; and assigns a definite

Example 3.1 Comparison of T-1

melodic pitch to each syllable, using no parlando and therefore minimizing the spoken element in her more musically oriented delivery.

Elsewhere in the piece Lu only occasionally uses parlando for narrative emphasis. By contrast, Xiao not only uses the more speech-oriented parlando at the outset, but also uses it liberally throughout the rest of the performance, creating a vocal flamboyance that is one of the hallmarks of the masculine Liu school. Conversely, where Xiao uses a style more akin to spoken language,

Example 3.2 Comparison of vocal styles in T-3, T-5, T-7

amplifying the linguistic tone with dramatic changes in pitch, Lu relies more on a melodic portrayal of linguistic tone and sings in a more legato style. A comparison of the two schools at lines T-3, T-5, and T-7 illustrates these differences (see Example 3.2). Additionally, Lu uses parlando sparingly at the end of T-5 on *jiubazhege* (gathers) for the sake of variety, and on *xuesheng* (student) in T-7 to indicate the young man's clumsy, uncontrolled movements—a kind of word painting.

Tonality

Lu also emphasizes the tonic much more than Xiao, who sometimes replaces the tonic with the supertonic, evidenced in a comparison of the beginning of T-4, the twelfth measure of B-4, and the seventh measure of B-6 (see Example 3.3).

Example 3.3 Comparison of the tonic vs. the supertonic

Ornamentation

Extended trills and aesthetic grace notes are also integral to the feminine Luo style of singing and are employed as a matter of course, as opposed to the masculine Liu style, which uses them much more sparingly. The more melodic nature of the Luo school is demonstrated by a comparison of the second and third measures of T-4; the second and third measures of T-6; and the first and second measures of T-9 (Example 3.4).

Metric regularity

The Luo school also emphasizes metric symmetry more than the Liu school. Both versions are sung in the rhythmic mode of "slow meter" (*manban*) (Lawson 2011:84–92), but only Lu maintains a strict sense of 4/4 meter throughout the piece. Xiao sometimes sings two-beat measures, as in the ninth and fourteenth measures of B-1; the sixth measure of B-4; and the seventh measure of B-7 (see Example 3.5).

Xiao also sings five-beat measures at the ends of T-3, T-8, and T-9, whereas Lu extends, abbreviates, and alters the melodic material to fit into four-beat

Example 3.4 Comparison of melodic rendering

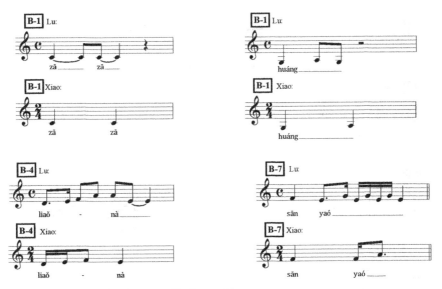

Example 3.5 Lu's four-beat vs. Xiao's two-beat measures

measures at all times in her rendition. In essence, Lu's version is characterized by more purely musical and formal concerns regarding melodic phrasing, metric regularity, and vocal ornamentation (Example 3.6).

Similarities between the styles

In keeping with the adage "first convey the text, then sing the tune" (*xian nianzi hou changqiang*), performers in both schools communicate the word tone of the lyrics as accurately as possible at the outset, while establishing their personal uniqueness as a singer.[10] By the ends of the lines and couplets, however, performers have communicated the basic information of the line or phrase and are not as beholden to linguistic tone as they are at the beginnings of lines,[11] so the performers of both schools freely employ musically recognizable elements or formulae common to both traditions (Lawson 2011: 88–93). These formulae represent a part of the piece where formal musical interests dominate, and the hummable, recognizable cadences lend continuity to pieces within the Beijing Drumsong tradition. The most dramatic example of similarity between the two versions is from B-9[1] to the end of the piece, representing the final cadential formula (see Example 3.7).

The essence of the female style

When comparing the two most prominent schools of Beijing Drumsong in the Tianjin Municipal *Quyi* Arts Troupe, it is clear that the feminine Luo

Example 3.6 Lu's four-beat vs. Xiao's five-beat measures

school features a more lyrical singing style than the masculine Liu school, and the parlando of the Liu school is replaced by definite melodic pitches. The Luo school features conjunct melodies, tonality that is more precisely defined around the tonic, and metric regularity throughout the piece. When combined, these characteristics of the Luo school move the vocal text further from the spoken language and more into the realm of singing, verifying the commonly used phrase used to describe the high degree of musicality in the Luo tradition, *yinyuehuale* ("musicalization"). The musicality of the Luo style in no way interfered with the audience's ability to comprehend the lyrics, and all my consultants agree that her vocal style actually enhances the appreciation of the lyrics, creating a perfect aesthetic balance between text and tune.

Example 3.7 Comparison of the final cadential formula

Luo's musical innovations coincided with the existing trend toward feminization (*nuxinghua*) that arose from the use of a female narrator, which was prevalent even before Luo Yusheng made dramatic changes in Beijing Drumsong.[12] The appearance of Xiao Lanyun, Zhang Cuifeng, and Sun Shujun—all female disciples of Liu Baoquan—verifies the ascendancy of female performers in the early decades of the twentieth century. Unlike her female contemporaries, who tried to emulate their male masters as closely as possible, albeit with their feminine voices,[13] Luo was not content to sing a male style in a feminine voice; instead, she enhanced the female voice by consciously creating a lyrical melodic style that suited the stories about metaphysical heroines. In the right place, at the right time, with the right vocal talent and the genius to know exactly how to employ her skills to her benefit, Luo Yusheng deliberately created a novel school of singing that also happened to be in sync with the increased approval of female participation in the public sphere.

Luo Yusheng is not simply known as one of the early female competitors in Tianjin *quyi*; she is referred to as the queen of drumsinging, and as an innovator on par with Liu Baoquan, the king of drumsinging. Her musical contributions to the genre ultimately affected female performers in other genres, contributing to the overall trend towards *yinyuehua* (musicalization) and its concomitant *nuxinghua* (feminization) in *quyi* performance (Xue 1985a). The China Record Company acknowledged her standing as one of the great vocal artists of the twentieth century by awarding her 1961 recording of "Listening to the Bells at Sword Pavilion" in 1989 with first prize, a rarity for a female singer. The following section analyzes her brilliant musical setting of her signature piece, whose text was examined at the end of Chapter 2.

Setting the text of "Listening to the Bells at Sword Pavilion"

To enhance the sheer power and beauty of the female voice, Luo used a new type of musical lyricism in singing stories about metaphysical heroines. The word "lyricism" is an especially appropriate term in this context because of its many shades of meaning between music and poetry. In poetry, "lyric" implies musical character; in music, "lyric" refers to the words of a song or a high register of the soprano voice. Because of the liminal relationship between text and tune in the Chinese vocal arts, Chinese poetry, as mentioned at the beginning of the chapter, is simultaneously musical and literary. As James Liu explains,

> the clear-cut quality of Chinese syllables, the absence of elision and liaison, and the fact that there are usually few syllables in each line, all tend to produce a *staccato* effect, unlike the more flowing *legato* rhythms of English or French verse.
>
> (1974: 38)

As a consequence, most Chinese poetry is chanted rather than read, and singing is merely the next step beyond chanting in navigating the space between poetry and music. By singing the text, the singer actually compensates for both the brevity and the staccato effect of the poetry.

But there is also another reason for the significance of setting Chinese poetry to music. As Herbert explains, "Music's frequent coupling with words ... makes it an effective medium for the processing of imagining, reminiscing and reflecting that may or may not possess a partially linguistic quality" (2011: 195). She continues by saying that, as a multimodal experience, music "can be conceptualized as a composite of different types of conscious and non-conscious experience ... any one of which may be more dominant at a certain moment" (2011: 195). "Listening" provides ample opportunities for this multimodality, taking the listener to a variety of different places between life and illusion, this world and the supernatural.

Along with the organic relationship between poetry and music and the capacity for musically rendered lyrics to provide multimodality for listeners in Chinese narratives, the melancholy story of "Listening" also suggests another reason for a musical setting: The story pleads for a female voice.[14] If "Bai Niu Tells a Story" glorifies the metaphysical feminine singing voice, then "Listening to the Bells at Sword Pavilion" petitions for the "grain" of its corporeal resonance. Singing this narrative poem gives an actual voice to the emperor's grief and guilt, and, more importantly, provides the missing voice of Lady Yang herself, especially when sung by a female narrator.

Unlike other adaptations of the story, a ghostly Yang Guifei neither appears nor speaks to the emperor in Luo's version of "Listening," a point that only reinforces the emperor's guilt and Lady Yang's sense of betrayal. Hence, if Lady Yang's story about her wrongful death is retold through a female narrator, it is as though Lady Yang's wounded spirit may be partially appeased. Zeitlin explains how illnesses (and we could consider the emperor's depressed state to be an illness) are sometimes considered the wages of sin, and so Lady Yang's absence is punitive, a case of waiting for her grievances to be properly redressed (2007: 46). A singing female narrator retelling the tale initiates a kind of reparation.

The significance of the female narrator's voice makes this story about a wronged female ghost particularly powerful for the performer. Basing my argument on Abbate's idea that certain musical moments have a special sonorous presence (1996: xiii), I suggest that the whole musical soliloquy of "Listening" is a therapeutic gesture that allows the narrator, acting as a medium who conjures up the past, to acknowledge the wrongs committed against the metaphysical heroine. In allowing Lady Yang to have an audible voice, the female narrator plays a role heretofore unavailable to women. Recognizing the power inherent in singing this piece, Luo Yusheng made this piece her masterwork (*daibiao zuopin*).[15]

Consisting of 38 couplets, "Listening" is a relatively short piece, compared to some drumsong pieces that contain over 140 couplets. But the markedly slow tempo and emphasis on musical and textual nuance results in a piece that ultimately takes as long to sing as pieces that have longer texts and are sung much more rapidly (Stevens 1975: 122). In order to appreciate the careful and deliberate musical rendition as it gives life to the text, I base my analysis on Poizat's three vocal levels in Western opera: enhancing the text, presenting the voice object, and witnessing the singer (outlined in Abbate 1996: 11).

Enhancing the text

The best way to appreciate the way music enhances the text is to read the full text and then listen to the complete musical performance.[16] By doing this, the reader-listener sees and hears how the piece comes to life in the same way a visitor experiences the visceral beauty of a scene after looking at a photograph. If a reader were to recite the syllables of "Listening," it would take no longer than seven minutes; however, as sung with the musical introduction and interlude, the piece takes a little longer than 16 minutes to perform. Hence, the act of singing fills out the rendition substantially, thereby compensating for the brevity and staccato nature of the poetry.

Most of the piece is sung in the lyrical melody (*pingqiang*), which provides the melodic framework for ornamenting the musical syllables according to an established musical formula (Stevens 1975: 137–178; Lawson 2011: 82–93). The first couplet of the text is given in Romanized syllables below, with

Example 3.8 Musical transcription of the first couplet of "Listening" in the lyrical melody

translation, followed by a transcription of the way the music both embellishes and savors the lyrics (in Example 3.8). This example is typical of Luo's vocal style throughout the majority of the piece. Note the delicately ornamented rendering of selected syllables in measures 27 (wei), 29 (cao), 30 (qing), 32 (jin), 33 (cun), and 36 (ling).

T-1 *Mawei po xia cao qing qing*
   (On the hillside of Mawei, where the grass is lush and green)
B-1 *Jin ri you cun fei zi ling*
   (The tomb of the concubine remains to this day)

The narrative melody (*shangban*) is added to the lyrical melody for the last section of the piece. Sung to a faster tempo, the only ornaments are single grace notes preceding textual syllables, which are used sparingly to create word tone. The free rhythm of the narrative melody—with only a regular pulse—creates a cadence that is more akin to speech than the measured and melodically elaborated vocalization of the rest of the piece. During this last section, the text is rendered plainly to wrap up the story with the clearest diction possible. Thus, the musical enhancement is minimal yet effective as a climax as it increases in tempo and volume. Example 3.9 demonstrates two of the last seven couplets of the final section.

The final example in which music enhances the text is in the instrumental introduction and interludes.[17] Originally, the drum introduction served as an advertisement for outdoor, rural performances, but as Beijing Drumsong became an urban phenomenon at teahouses and theaters in the early twentieth century (Stevens 1975: 81), the introduction functioned as a time of

Example 3.9 Couplets 36 and 37 of "Listening" in the narrative melody (akin to speech)

preparation for both singer and audience. Herbert says that "music, through its internal organization, can effectively disrupt temporal synchronicity, allowing the perceiver temporarily to stand outside clock time via entrainment to a different time frame" (2011:197), and the introduction interrupts temporality with the beginning of a story, an alternate reality.

While it might seem counter-intuitive to consider instrumental portions as enhancing the words of the piece, the non-singing musical sections serve to frame the drama and underscore both the previous and subsequent sung portions, allowing audiences to both ponder and anticipate the story. Herbert explains that music can offer "a freedom from verbal language—an alternative mental 'space' where the interaction between perceiver and stimulus does not have to constitute an effortful decoding of informationally precise meaning" (2011: 196). Given the difficulty of the semi-literary lyrics, short interludes between sections provide a brief respite for the singer and an opportunity for the audience to contemplate the story thus far. For example, the longest interlude, of 16 measures (mm. 144–160 in Appendix 5), occurs after the first third of the performance. This interlude gives the singer time to rest before the most challenging part of the story and gives the audience an opportunity to reflect on the plot, the imagery, the lyrics, and the beauty of the vocal rendition.

Presenting the voice object

Ostensibly, in the Chinese narrative arts, music should not dominate the text, and no performer would ever claim otherwise. But the reality of performance reveals a tension between the text and the voice object. Traditionally, performers would circulate written texts of new pieces among members of the audience before a performance (Stevens 1990: 70–71), and today supertitles are used in live performances; and subtitles in televised performances, to ensure linguistic comprehension, arguably because of the expectation that the voice occasionally usurps the power of the written word. Abbate claims that music "has the capacity to assail us with its sheer sound," communicating "both with and *across* the text, furnishing us with the opportunity to hear many narrating voices (both textual and musical)" (1996: ix, xiv).[18] She explains that the musical capacity to assail the listener with sound is sometimes manifested in voices that behave as "a rare and peculiar *act*, a unique moment of performing narration within a surrounding music" (1996: 19). Despite the high premium placed on the literary element in Chinese narratives, there are instances of such usurping moments in "Listening." Indeed, these acts represent what Poizat calls the "voice object" (1992: 33–34), and their presence in performance signifies the Chinese penchant for exploring the liminal space between music and language.

According to Poizat, the voice object often becomes the primary focus for the listener in Western opera. In the same way, the voice object in Beijing Drumsong can also sometimes compete with the lyrics for the audience's attention. The transcription in Example 3.10, of T-10 at the end of section two, is such an example: *chang xu duan tan (a)* (the emperor sighs deeply). In measures 129–135 the non-lexical "*a*" (in parentheses) is sung to an especially long melody that represents one of the musical and emotional high-points of the entire piece. At this moment, Luo is allowing the emperor to sigh audibly as a visceral manifestation of his grief. While this emotional melody does indeed enhance the meaning of the text, Luo's temporary melismatic flight from the lyrics still expresses the semantic meaning and, at the same time, allows the music to enhance the pathos of the sigh.

Although such melisma can add a meaningful dimension to the lyrics, musical ornamentation can occasionally interfere with linguistic comprehension. I have argued elsewhere about the balance between musical ornamentation and linguistic comprehension in *quyi* genres (Lawson 2011: 73–76, 86–93), but it is worth mentioning this point once again in the context of a genre where the text holds such importance. For example, while the melody in Example 3.11 creates word tone accurately at the outset of each syllable, the melodies become ornamented enough with "filler words" that the normally contiguous syllables are separated: see especially after *hun* and *zi* in measure 182; *liang* and *gu* in 185; *di* in 186; *er* in 187; and *wo* in 188. According to Abbate, such melismatic singing separates syllables, splits words, and can destroy language (1996: 10–11). In this Beijing Drumsong piece, however,

Example 3.10 A musical sigh at the end of T-10

Example 3.11 T-13 and B-13: Splitting syllables with post-lexical elongations

Luo's ornamented singing does not destroy language. After each syllable has been correctly executed according to word tone, the melismas underscore another level of meaning through word painting at this poignant part of the drama: "*dang lang lang—the frightening sounds from the eaves approach in the front, as the bone-rattling cold rises from the depths of the quilt.*" The musical rendering enhances the meaning in a way that mere reading or reciting could never accomplish. For example, in measure 182 after *jing hun* (frightening) and *zi* (from the eaves), and in measures 184 to 185 after *bing* (ice), the second *liang* (cold), and *gu* (bone); the melismas accentuate the meanings of those individual words—despite the fact that the syllables are separated (see Example 3.11).

Although these musical moments may temporarily disrupt the normal rhythms of language, they are never distracting enough to obscure the meaning of the text. Luo's genius was in the balancing of text and tune. While circulating a script among traditional patrons or providing super- or subtitles for modern audiences is an acknowledgement that the musical rendition might at times overshadow the text, the compelling reason for coming to a performance is not to read; it is to hear and witness the musical rendition of story, with all the inherent tensions between the lyrics and melody.

Despite some places in the performance where musical concerns offer a subtle challenge to linguistic ones, the relationship between language and music in Chinese narratives is much more congenial than it is in Western opera. Poizat explains that music in Western opera may draw audiences away from the words, creating a "radical automization" for the voice object that commands the attention of the audience (1992: 33). In the Chinese narrative context, the physical and sensual presence of musical sound, even as it occasionally moves away from the lyrics that embed it, ultimately presents the complementary union of two opposing forces. Music and language are simultaneously appreciated as audience members teeter between the musical and the linguistic when the two elements are constantly being recreated in performance. The liminal tension between elegant lyrics and the beauty of the voice-object constitutes the great allure for a Chinese aficionado.

While Luo's classic version of "Listening" is a brilliant example of the feminization of *quyi* in musically rendering texts, other sung genres in Tianjin *quyi* also developed due to the musical contributions of female narrators. The enjoyment of hearing beautiful texts set to music is considered the greatest pleasure in all of the sung genres, but the fact that sung poetry became a mode of feminine expression for the women of *quyi* is arguably one of the most significant developments in Tianjin *quyi*. Abu-Lughod states that poetry, as an artistic endeavor, "reminds people of another way of being and encourages, as it reflects, another side of experience" (1999: 259). I would add that the language and structure of *sung* poetry is particularly significant for the women of *quyi*, as it reflects their own feminine experience. Female narrators in Tianjin were both curators of the texts drawn from traditional folklore and semi-classical literature as well as innovators of a new singing style that featured a treble voice. Their contributions constituted an example of Butler's idea of iteration with a difference (1997: 7). The difference, in this case, is a feminized musical discourse.

Notes

1 See Lawson (2011: 47–56, 131–132) for more information about the tonal nature of Chinese and the implications of linguistic tone for setting texts to music in the narrative arts.
2 For more detailed analysis of the musical "weightiness" (*yinyuexing hen qiang*) of this genre, see Lawson (2011: 59–76).
3 Jonathan Stock also makes the point that enhancing musical aspects distinguishes

female singers (and female impersonators) from singers of male roles in *Huju* opera in modern Shanghai (2003: 86–96).

4 By the time Luo Yusheng had decided to study Beijing Drumsong, there were actually three schools: The Liu school (*Liupai*), after Liu Baoquan (1868–1942); the Bai school (*Baipai*), after Bai Yunpeng (1874–1952); and the second Bai school (*shao Baipai*), after Bai Fengming (1909–1980). Luo Yusheng began her studies with Liu Baoquan's accompanist ("string master") Han Yonglu (1876–1943), who knew intimately the musical differences among the three schools. Han brought together the best features of all three styles when he taught Luo, and she was able to benefit from his eclectic pedagogy as she developed her own school. See Tao Dun (1983: 69) and Liu Shufang (1983: 94–103) for a discussion about the performers and teachers who influenced Luo Yusheng's musical development.

5 See Stevens (1975, 1991) for more about Zhang (Jang) and Sun as early female performers of Beijing Drumsong.

6 While a complete analysis of both versions would include a study of the instrumental passages, the present analysis focuses solely on a comparison of the vocal renditions of the two singers. See Stevens (1975: 238–241) for an English translation of "At Break of Day," and Lawson (2011: 145–158) for a musical transcription of Lu's version of the entire piece.

7 I was able to access an unmarked cassette tape of a radio performance of this short piece performed by Xiao Lanyun, recorded some time when she was a mature woman.

8 Lu Yiqin allowed me to record her singing this piece during a rehearsal. The entire performance is available on track 3 of the CD included in Lawson 2011.

9 I have adopted Stevens's convention for indicating the top and bottom lines of the couplets as "T" and "B," respectively (1975: 104–136).

10 See Lawson (2011: 82–93) for more information on singing word tone in Beijing Drumsong.

11 Once the most important linguistic information is conveyed at the beginning of the line, the performer can allow musical considerations to take over.

12 The feminization of genres took place in Tianjin Popular Tunes, Beijing Drumsong, Tambourine Drumsong (*Danxiar*), Pear Blossom Drumsong (*Lihuadagu*), Plum Blossom Drumsong (*Meihuadagu*), and other sung genres as well.

13 See Stevens (1975: 50) for an interesting anecdote about Liu trying to get Zhang to sing with more feminine gestures.

14 For a full translation of this text, see Chapter 2.

15 See Nan and Qian (1999: 48) describing Luo first hearing, at age 12, "Listening" performed by Pear Blossom Drumsong (*Lihuadagu*) singer Dong Lianzhi—an experience that left a deep impression on her.

16 I have included the Chinese text and my musical transcription of Luo's classic 1961 performance of "Listening" in appendices 3 and 5, respectively. Winning first prize in 1989 for her 1961 rendition of her signature work places Luo Yusheng in the same league as other recipients such as Mei Lanfang, Hou Baolin, Liu Baoquan, and other legendary Chinese performers. See Zhao 2012 to hear the first few verses of this performance on a program rebroadcasted by Beijing Television (BTV) in 2012 on the tenth anniversary of Luo's death.

17 Please refer to the following passages in Appendix 5: measures 1–26 for the introduction; and 66–79, 144–160, 231–244, and 349–360 for the interludes.

18 As mentioned in Chapter 2, Abbate's ideas emerge from her research on Western opera. Despite the obvious differences between Western opera and Chinese *quyi*, the general notion of an inherent tension between voice and text is comparable between the two genres.

4 Liminal Voices

Transferring Artistry from Master to Disciple

The blue color extracted from the indigo plant is bluer than the plant it comes from.

Chinese Proverb

The result is that the B character, supposedly the less assertive and talkative of the two, actually takes on a role equal to that of the A character as he argues vehemently for the importance of his "supportive" persona.

David Moser (1990: 59)

If, as Jon McKenzie (2001: 49) asserts, the field of performance studies is deliberately positioned as liminal, occupying the space between ritual and theater, then the performance of pedagogical relationships in Tianjin *quyi* is an apt example of this liminality. The disciplined rituals that initiate the relationship between a *shifu* (master teacher) and her *tudi* (disciple)[1] eventually give way to unbridled theater when the latter first challenges her master's dominance. In my research on the following select group of female narrators, I discovered that transferring the skills associated with coveted female vocality is a highly charged, emotionally taxing process.

Disciples invariably experience conflict, in a manner that recalls to Julia Kristeva's notion of abjection,[2] when they try to establish themselves as independent artists. In discussing how children experience trauma when they try to break free of their mothers, Julia Kristeva claims that "abjection is above all ambiguity. Because, while releasing a hold, it does not radically cut off the subject from what threatens it—on the contrary, abjection acknowledges it to be in perpetual danger" (Kristeva 1982: 9). Elaborating on this point, Barbara Creed explains, "The position of the child is rendered even more unstable because, while the mother retains a close hold over the child, [the relationship] can serve to authenticate her existence—an existence which needs validation" (Creed 2007: 11–12). As the child breaks away, the mother becomes an "abject" if she refuses to surrender her hold on the child. A similar problem occurs if the child does not break away, and chooses the security of the relationship over independence and autonomy.

Such is also the dilemma of disciples and masters, who experience a kind of secondary abjection—a replication of the primary maternal abjection—as adults who struggle with breaking the bonds established by female masters and their disciples. Yet the antagonism intrinsic to the changing nature of master–disciple relationships, which are seemingly doomed to implode from the outset, is essential to the longevity of the art form of *quyi* the same way that the trauma of abjection is necessary to human development. Barry Jean Ancelet explains the ways that performers navigate their changing statuses by arguing that reconfiguring roles is necessary for the sake of preserving and regenerating the institution (2007: 172). To paraphrase Judith Butler, one's status as a master or disciple is, of necessity, constantly being re-negotiated through various acts of performance (Butler 2007: 187), implying that Bai Niu herself could eventually be challenged by her protégée, Hei Niu.[3]

This chapter outlines several concrete examples of the ways adult females work through a type of abjection as they try to create their own voices and establish themselves in careers apart from their masters within the community I studied in Tianjin. Drucilla Cornell states that Kristeva's discourses on the centrality of motherhood do not provide examples of feminine creativity beyond the maternal (1991: 72), but the case studies in this chapter demonstrate adult female creativity in the wake of the secondary abjection associated with master–disciple relationships.

Apprentices and disciples

In order to grasp the significance of female discipleship, it is important to understand the kind of pedagogy that the women of *quyi* in Tianjin inherited from the practice of apprenticeship in the artisanal industries. In many of the developing industries in Tianjin during the first half of the twentieth century, apprentices made up a significant part of the workforce. Under most circumstances, apprenticeship in Tianjin lasted for approximately three years and provided room, board, and job training after the first year for young males between the ages of 14 and 18 (Hershatter 1986: 52). Hershatter explains that:

> In twentieth-century Tianjin, however, apprenticeship was less a means of protecting craftsman status than a disguised form of child labor. Apprentices were not guaranteed training in a skill. Many of the apprentices who worked long hours in Tianjin shops were unable to find employment as craftsmen when they completed their apprenticeships. Shop owners preferred to acquire a new batch of apprentices, who were cheaper and easier to control.
>
> (1986: 52)

Like other young people in Tianjin, *quyi* entertainers were considered to be workers, and the training of new *quyi* performers bore some basic similarities to the system employed by artisans. For example, the usual tenure of a *quyi* novice was three years and three months, and, like the system for artisans, training in the *quyi* community entailed a type of slave labor that generated revenue for teachers (Xue 1985a). However, unlike artisans, who had the stamina, time, and financial resources to train multiple apprentices, *quyi* masters were much more limited in their resources; their apprentices would more accurately be termed as disciples. The living performance tradition that bound both master and disciple to the greater performance community required that disciples learn from respected, credentialed performers in order to establish themselves firmly in the musical and social network, and master teachers were compelled to acquire disciples in order to ensure the continuation of their musical heritage (Xue 1985b). Because of the nature of the commitment between master and disciple, a master performer traditionally invested heavily in the training of selected disciples in order to produce successors worthy of the tradition. It was important to encourage disciples to be as successful as possible because if a disciple were especially talented, she could earn a significant amount of money for the master during the ~~training~~ period of training and would continue to have the responsibility to carry on the master's name after gaining her independence (Xue 1985b).

The traditional master–disciple relationship in Tianjin *quyi* is inherently more complex, fluid, and enduring than the artisan–apprentice relationship, and disciples must become proficient at employing a repertoire of social behaviors to elevate their status. Performers tacitly recognize that a disciple's subordinate position implies both an important hidden power vis-à-vis the master teacher and a base from which to negotiate that power, thereby potentially subverting the hierarchy. The machinations of masters and disciples reveal the professional conflicts and interpersonal negotiations associated with secondary abjection.

Because of their unique vocal training, I argue that the women of *quyi* felt empowered to challenge boundaries in ways that elite women or underclass women with no skills could not; this power is especially evident in the way they manipulated their relationships as disciples vis-à-vis their masters.

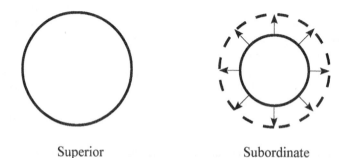

Superior   Subordinate

Figure 4.1 A subordinate position implies hidden power and a base from which to negotiate that power

Despite their tenuous upbringings, the lowborn women of *quyi* achieved greatness by utilizing the two major tactics of a negotiating strategy called *guanxi*:[4] (1) currying favor to improve one's status and (2) withholding favor to curtail another's status.[5] Assuming either a superior or subordinate role involves both tactics at key points in master–disciple relationships. While people in all cultures employ similar strategies, the uniqueness of Chinese *guanxi* is found in the way that its tactics are embodied symbolically in theatrical performance and in the way it is accepted—grudgingly and sometimes contemptuously—as an inexorable law in social interaction.

Role types in comic routines: Keys to master–disciple relationships

The way power is negotiated in master–disciple relationships is remarkably well explained by a close analysis of role types in the *quyi* genre known as Comic Routines (*xiangsheng*).[6] Using Turner and Turner's (2007: 323) notion about the dynamic interdependence between cultural performances and social interactions, the following discussion likens the fictive, on-stage relationships between the role types in Comic Routines (*xiangsheng*) to similar patterns used by female masters and disciples in navigating their social and professional relationships.

Male actors exclusively perform the roles in Comic Routines, but this in no way diminishes the usefulness of these role types for understanding the social machinations of female performers. As Harris and Pease explain, understanding the importance of social gender over anatomical sex is a recurrent theme in the literature about Chinese performance (2013: 10). Moreover, since male authors freely use female archetypes in their literary works and female impersonators became famous for portraying female characters, the commutability of gender is already well established in Chinese literature and performance. The fluid boundaries between male and female allow for free-flowing exchanges in ideas and practices, and, in this case, applying male roles in stage performance to female roles in social performance illuminates broader patterns of master–disciple relationships. The patterns of interaction between superiors and subordinates exemplify the struggles connected with secondary abjection in negotiating changes in relationships.

Within the first several months of conducting research in Tianjin, I was fortunate to learn about Comic Routines (*xiangsheng*) from Professor Xue Baokun, a respected scholar in Chinese vernacular literature at Nankai University in Tianjin (Xue 1985a, 1985b, 1985c). Two male actors usually perform Comic Routines, each of whom memorizes carefully scripted parts written by authors trained in Chinese vernacular literature and social satire. The subordinate character in Comic Routines wields a great deal of power in the performance relationship.[7] If the subordinate actor were to withhold his support of the dominant actor in any way (one of the *guanxi* tactics), the latter would be unable to perform.[8] Watching the unfolding of the relationship between the dominant comedic actor—the *dougende*—and the supportive "straight man"—the *penggende*—in Comic Routines is highly entertaining and surprisingly revelatory. As Xue Baokun explained the fictive performance relationships between the two actors, he also suggested that the patterns of interaction described in Comic Routines exemplify other types of relationships in general social intercourse.

Writers of Comic Routines usually manipulate the relationship between these two roles in one of two ways, the *yitouchen* and the *zimugen* styles. In the *yitouchen* or "heavy on one end" style, the *dougende* is the dominant actor to the *penggende*. Although the *dougende* is ostensibly perceived as playing the superior role, the *penggende* is essential to the success of the entire performance.

A more equal relationship between these two roles exists in the second major type of Comic Routines known as the *zimugen* or "two sides of a snap"

Comic Routines
Xiangsheng

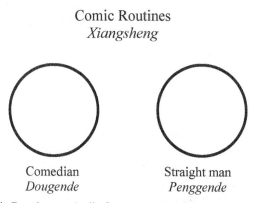

Comedian · *Dougende*   Straight man · *Penggende*

Figure 4.2 Comic Routines typically feature a comedian (*dougende*) and a straight man (*penggende*)

Yitouchen
"Heavy on one end"

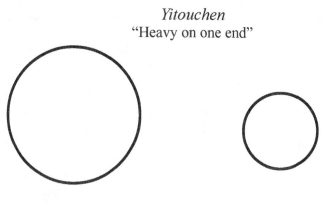

Dougende   *Penggende*

Figure 4.3 In the *yitouchen* (heavy on one end) style, the *dougende* is seemingly superior to the *penggende*

Zimugen
"Two sides of a snap"

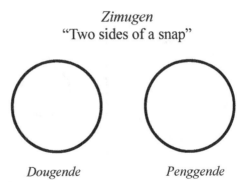

Dougende   *Penggende*

Figure 4.4 In the *zimugen* (two sides of a snap) style, the *dougende* and *penggende* are equal

style, which features a more equal and balanced interaction between the *dougende* and the *penggende*.

Writers of Comic Routines pride themselves on the subtle experimentation of all of the possible ways for communicating through the *dougende* and the *penggende* in both the *yitouchen* and *zimugen* styles of Comic Routines.[9] Moreover, the various permutations of the *dougende* and the *penggende* constitute an artistic embodiment of the fluidity implied in interpersonal associations on a more general social level.[10] For example, the first phase of a relationship between two individuals usually involves assuming *dougende*- and *penggende*-like roles according to an *yitouchen*-like system of ranking into superior and subordinate positions. However, in these social situations, a superior or subordinate status is not permanent; social roles are in a constant state of transformation in liminal space, depending upon changes in the lives of each individual in relation to his or her colleagues. Implicit in all relationships is an *expectation* for change and an understanding that possibilities for upward mobility for the subordinate are inherent in this system. What may begin as an *yitouchen* relationship can often evolve into a more *zimugen* type of relationship, where the subordinate—as the symbolic *penggende*—eventually becomes more powerful to the point where the two performers relate as equals.

While the variability of superior–subordinate relationships applies to male members of the society and to mixed gender settings, an understanding of the flexibility inherent in social roles is helpful in expanding an awareness of Tianjin female narrators as highly capable in navigating social and professional relationships. Female narrators not only occupy positions of influence with respect to both men and women, but they also possess a power similar to the *penggende* when they assume a subordinate position to a more powerful male or female colleague. Despite changes in pedagogical institutions since 1949 (Lawson 2011: 23–30), the relationship between master and disciple

Yitouchen

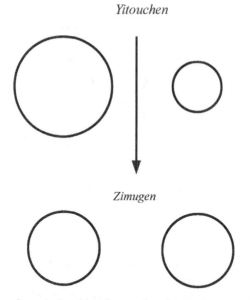

Zimugen

Figure 4.5 An *yitouchen* relationship often evolves into a *zimugen* relationship

continues to be an essential part of the development of Tianjin *quyi*, and yet, as mentioned, it is fraught with antagonism.[11]

Given the inherent conflict in the master–disciple relationship, one might ask why a student would even want to become a female narrator. In the first half of the twentieth century, a disciple usually sought a master because it was the only means by which she could become a professional performer. Today, however, students do not seek masters for the same reasons. From about 1970 to 1985, the troupe solicited students to train in groups, thereby de-emphasizing the traditional master–disciple relationship. Since 1986, the Academy for Northern *Quyi* (*Zhongguo beifang Quyi xuexiao*) assumes the primary responsibility for training all prospective singers, accompanists, and writers, and also ostensibly de-emphasizes the bond between student and artist (Lawson 2011: 28–29). Even though the need for masters is no longer apparent, a promising student still frequently seeks a master in order to have an older and more experienced ally in the community. In a world where awards are bestowed both because of individual merit and political connections within the *quyi* community, a disciple is at a distinct advantage by having a master with a wide network of contacts. A student who was trained solely by the troupe or the academy does not get the individual attention that a disciple would get from a master who assumes personal responsibility for the disciple's success. A disciple is also looked upon more favorably in the community when she has formed a traditional alliance with a master performer. Establishing this relationship is viewed as a way of paying homage to artistic heritage—a rite in which the entire community celebrates in the richness of local traditions.[12]

The master's desire for a disciple is even more compelling. As discussed previously, having a disciple meant an economic advantage for the master, as she could demand all of the disciple's wages while under her tutelage. More importantly, the master could gain professional advantage by having artistic progeny. Disciples were viewed like male children within a Chinese family, and the more disciples a master has, the more respected her school of performance. However, a master may be afraid of the disciple becoming proficient, thereby threatening the performer's monopoly on the genre. This is the weak link of this arrangement: The master–disciple relationship fails both when a disciple is incapable of completing her training and when she surpasses her master. For this reason, a master usually wants as many disciples as possible, and tries to turn them into become replicas of herself (Xue 1986a).[13] A master will often want only limited success for the disciple as an imitator and will try to curtail her development beyond a certain level of proficiency, and the master may consider the disciple a complete failure on the grounds that the latter has not succeeded in becoming proficient in the style. In one sense, the perception that all students have failed exalts the master's position as a singer without peers—an *yitouchen*-like figure.

Nevertheless, the symbolic value of both masters and disciples far outweighs any other considerations. Young performers who are anxious to excel continue to look for advantageous alliances with master performers, and master performers are acutely aware of the need to preserve their legacy by having many disciples. Creed explains the following point in her analysis of Kristeva's notion of abjection—a point relevant to this discussion about disciples (as subjects) and masters (as abjects): "Although the subject must exclude the abject, the abject must, nevertheless, be tolerated for that which threatens to destroy life also helps to define it" (2007: 9). Simultaneously tolerating and excluding the abject is, indeed, one of the ironies associated with the master–disciple relationship.

Examples of master–disciple relationships among the women of *Quyi*

The following case studies are composites of three types of master–disciple relationships among members of the Tianjin Municipal *Quyi* Arts Troupe. It is rare to find a master–disciple relationship that is not antagonistic on some level. In general, however, female masters and disciples are adept at navigating these relationships to their professional benefit. As mentioned in note 3 of the Prologue, I have changed the names and superficial details in each account to ensure the anonymity of my consultants. I have also put their words in italics in order to distinguish them from my own analysis, which is printed in regular type.

Case One: An intense rivalry between master and disciple

Master Jiang, an elderly singer, is a retired member of the Tianjin Municipal *Quyi* Arts Troupe. She achieved excellence as a performer and as a leader in spite of the burdens she faced as a young child from an impoverished family. Ji, Jiang's *da dizi* (first, oldest disciple), recounts the following story about Master Jiang:[14]

> *As a teenager, Master Jiang came into contact with drumsinging by meet-ing Mr. An Li, an influential performer of the sanxian*[15] *who had spent years accompanying many of the greatest drumsingers. An was anxious to find disciples to whom he could pass on his artistic tradition. When he discovered Jiang, he was particularly pleased because her voice was excep-tionally beautiful, and both her upper and lower registers were equally resonant—an important quality for a performer in the narrative arts.*
>
> *By her late twenties, Jiang had enjoyed considerable success as a per-former and she was anxious to begin the process of training someone to carry on her tradition. Up to this point, it was not yet common for female performers to solicit disciples, however, so Jiang decided to adopt a female child whom she could train unofficially. Because my family was under tre-mendous financial strain and since I would end up getting married and leaving home anyway, my family felt pressured to sell me. For that reason I was recommended to Jiang and she adopted me as her daughter.*

Hershatter explains that among the underclass in early twentieth-century Tianjin, "a girl was still regarded as a 'money-losing product' (*peiqianhuo*), since there was little possibility of her bringing enough income to the family to compensate for the food she ate" (1986: 80). Ji recognized that she was precisely that kind of burden on her natal family.

A surplus of lowborn female children can supply a demand for potential female singers among working-class performers, and this scenario made Ji's adoption a viable arrangement for all parties concerned. Ji's natal family benefitted from sending the daughter they could no longer afford to feed into an environment in which she was needed, Jiang adopted a child who could learn her art form, and Ji had the opportunity to develop a career. This situa-tion is an interesting twist on the familiar theme in the social science literature on the Chinese family, as in most instances, the Chinese prefer to have sons. Wolf explains,

In times past, many grandsons was not only a sign of a prosperous family, it often was the cause of that family's prosperity. Aside from being a support to their parents in their old age, sons were a father's legacy to the future of the family they had inherited from their fathers. (1985: 248)

From Jiang's perspective, however, it was imperative that she have a female child to whom she could pass on the uniquely feminine traits of her vocal style. Ji explains:

> *While Master Jiang had actually already given birth to a son, which is normally cause for great celebration among the Chinese, she chose to cul-tivate a parental and professional relationship with me. This bond between*

Master Jiang and me prevented her from establishing close parental ties with her biological son, who was raised instead by a nurse.

I studied singing with Master Jiang from age 14 to 17. However, since I was Jiang's adopted daughter, she felt that I would not be recognized as a respected member of the narrative arts community unless I formally became the disciple of another master. Consequently, she arranged for a distinguished accompanist by the name of Chen Benli to become my master. This token arrangement with Chen was calculated to give me the standing I needed in the community to become a professional, and yet I would still maintain my relationship with Master Jiang as both daughter and unofficial student.

Up to this point, Jiang was unquestionably superior to Ji as a performer, and therefore held a position of authority. However, when Ji was given an opportunity to study at the newly established Music Worker's Troupe (*Yinyue Gongzuo Tuan*) in Beijing when she turned 18, their relationship began to change. Ji continues:

Master Jiang no longer had control over my musical development as she had during the previous several years, and our singing styles diverged radically. When I eventually returned to Tianjin after my stay in Beijing, our relationship began to decline. Master Jiang no longer included me among her coterie of friends and patrons, and she also prevented me from using the best accompanists, keeping them for herself.

After the founding of the People's Republic in 1949, changes in the government placed new strains on their relationship. After the Communist Party began to restructure the arts and entertainment industries, Jiang and Ji became separate individuals in the eyes of the government. Even though they were already competitors by this point, the new government did not recognize their relationship as mother and daughter, so their rivalry intensified.

In the early 1980s, the practice of formally accepting disciples was reinstituted as part of the post-Cultural Revolution renaissance of Chinese social and cultural institutions. This was particularly significant for female performers. In the first half of the twentieth century, women were still in the process of establishing themselves as artists in the narrative arts community and did not normally solicit disciples. During the extreme period of socialism from about 1949 to 1980, both male and female performers were strongly discouraged from having disciples. However, since 1980, the traditional ceremony marking the master–disciple relationship (*baishihui*) has once again been reinstituted as a means for recognizing the importance of establishing artistic genealogies, and, for the first time, women have been actively encouraged to solicit disciples.[16] As a result, female performers have been especially anxious to attract as many disciples as possible in order to establish their legacy and legitimize their performance style. Jiang had already recognized the need for a female heir when she arranged to adopt Ji, even though Ji had not been considered a disciple at the time.

The changes in pedagogy from 1949 to 1980 did not remove the necessity of master–disciple ties—it intensified it. Both male and female performers have sought to make their mark by training disciples, as the prestige associated with having numerous disciples is not unlike the desire of a Chinese family to have as many sons as possible. Part of the perceived power of a master performer is dependent upon having many disciples, and the power of the disciple to influence the life and career of the master is similar to the great power of the *penggende*. Ji explains:

> *Even though social circumstances had prevented her from doing so, the fact that Master Jiang had not trained a disciple during the course of her career became embarrassingly apparent when the narrative arts community organized a celebration in her honor in 1983. Although everyone knew that Jiang had personally trained me and taught many other performers in the troupe, these people were considered merely students as opposed to formal disciples. People would often talk about Performer X having so many disciples and Person Y having so many disciples. Master Jiang was really embarrassed by this, because in so many other ways she was superior to most other performers. As a consequence, Master Jiang became understandably anxious to do something about this perceived deficiency. She persuaded an administrative cadre from the troupe to approach me to ask if I would agree to become her disciple.*
>
> *At first, I was taken aback by the request because I had already established that relationship with Mr. Chen.[17] Besides, I had always understood that as an adopted daughter I could not be considered Master Jiang's disciple. In the final analysis, I felt that there was nothing to gain from changing my relationship with her.[18]*
>
> *A year later, I was approached once again. This time I was told that Lin Zhenpei, a woman in the Northeast China Narrative Arts Troupe, wanted to become Jiang's disciple. I was informed that if I did not also agree to become Master Jiang's disciple, Lin Zhenpei would not pursue the issue— ostensibly because Lin did not want to displace me as the potential senior disciple.*
>
> *With this additional pressure, and with a measure of added reluctance, I finally consented. I assumed that Master Jiang wanted to change our relationship for two reasons: she would clearly maintain a position of authority over my career, and she would gain more respect in the narrative arts community since the title "master" implies more prestige than the title "mother." Shortly after the second request, I became Master Jiang's disciple, along with Lin Zhenpei and Liu Meiyan, a student whom Master Jiang had taught for several years during the early 1960s, in a ceremony held in the presence of dignitaries in the narrative arts community of Tianjin. Having successfully acquired three official disciples, Master Jiang contin-*

ued her efforts to attract additional disciples until she became too sick and infirm to teach.

While the goal of the master is to train disciples to replicate faithfully the master's tradition in an *yitouchen*-like fashion, the goal of the disciple is eventually to become an independent artist in her own right by developing her own style of singing and repertoire. In some instances, the disciple can become so popular that she exceeds her master in popularity, reflecting the oft-quoted proverb: "The blue color extracted from the indigo plant is bluer than the plant it comes from."

Master Jiang has always feared Ji because of her potential as a rival, and has tried to manipulate Ji's career whenever possible. Ji's unique style within the Jiang school set her apart from her teacher and won her a following independent of Master Jiang. Ji's successful tour to Canada, for example, has given her added ammunition in their ongoing competition for artistic supremacy, since Jiang's touring itinerary never extended beyond the borders of Hong Kong. Ji recognized hidden dimensions of her own *penggende*-like power as a subordinate when she contemplated Master Jiang's desperate attempt to acquire disciples in 1983. Since becoming Jiang's official disciple, Ji has been able to manipulate that power in various ways. Ji is well aware that when she refuses to participate in various concerts or functions that are important for Jiang's career, Jiang loses face in the community. While their relationship would still be characterized as *yitouchen*,[19] it represents an evolution in the direction towards as *zimugen* relationship that involves greater power for the subordinate.[20]

Case Two: A master without a disciple

The sharp tension in the relationship between Jiang and Ji is characteristic of two performers who are constantly contesting the hierarchy. This second case study reveals a different kind of tension between two singers, Master Wei and Zhu Min, whose conflict results from the fact that a master–disciple relationship was never established.

In the communication I have had with performers, connoisseurs, and leaders in the *quyi* community, I have rarely heard anything but admiration and respect for the artistry of Master Wei. She has no rivals because no one has ever come close to approximating her ability to sing her genre of *quyi*. She was popular as a young performer in the forties and fifties; as an innovator in the sixties and seventies; as a mature artist in the eighties and nineties; and as a retired legend up to the present day.

Master Wei was raised in her natal family. She recounts the following about the early stages of her career.

My older sister was the first to try and learn, but because she always got terrible stage fright, she never pursued singing seriously. When I started to learn to sing, however, I relished the opportunity to perform on stage, so my father encouraged me. My older brother was also a magician and, together as a family, we performed at small teahouses and theaters to earn extra money during the late 1930s and early 1940s.

At the height of my early career in the mid-1940s, I was singing three times a day, going from one theater to another in downtown Tianjin. At that time, female performers already outnumbered male performers among professionals in my genre. Women were preferred because men's voices were no good for this genre—there just wasn't anything exceptional about the sound of men singing. So the male performers ended up singing outdoors and in low-class theaters. They often sang the kind of texts that were coarse and vulgar. You see, theaters were ranked in those days. Only the best female performers were hired to sing at the most prestigious theaters where the more educated patrons came to hear artistically rendered pieces of relatively high literary quality. Many of the other female performers were either prostitutes or women from poor families who knew some of the pornographic texts that prostitutes sang. I never sang those texts because I wanted to be associated with the best performers.

I never really expected that I would pursue a career as a performer. I thought I would just get married and start a new life of my own. When I eventually married, however, my husband was an amateur lyricist and connoisseur of quyi, *and he actively encouraged me to continue to sing by writing new pieces for me.*

After 1949, Master Wei was recognized as one of the most accomplished performers of *quyi* in Tianjin, and she eventually became responsible for most of the vocal and instrumental innovations in the genre. Her singing style became the standard by which all others were measured. She had no official master, but a combination of native talent and early performance opportunities catapulted her to stardom. No one has ever come close to achieving the perfection of Master Wei's performance style, and everyone recognizes her unquestionable dominance.

As a respected and accomplished singer, Master Wei has been a member of the most prestigious troupe in the city, the winner of numerous national and local awards, and an instructor at the Academy for Northern Chinese Narrative Arts. Even though she retired in the early 1980s, she continued to perform until about the late 1990s. The only major source of dissatisfaction I have ever been able to sense about her career, which she rarely spoke about directly, concerns the issue of discipleship. Wei has trained many students over the years, but no one has ever emerged as a disciple. Her first students in the late 1950s were three young women, none of whom became good enough to perform professionally and are currently engaged in other professions. In the early 1970s, the Tianjin Municipal *Quyi* Arts Troupe recruited two young teenage girls to study with Wei. Several years later, three more girls were brought in. After their voices changed, however, only one of the three,

Zhu Min, showed any professional promise. Several young men were also recruited, but suffered a similar fate when their voices changed.

Unlike her classmates, Zhu Min continued to develop a beautiful voice after puberty, and she was officially designated as Wei's student by the Troupe—the first one for Wei after being a member of the Troupe for nearly 20 years. However, while Zhu was a gifted vocalist, she did not get along well with Wei because Zhu wanted to develop a different singing style from Wei. The strain in their relationship is apparent even today, despite having separate careers for the past 20 years. At all the functions where Wei is honored, Zhu rarely attends, and Wei does not speak about Zhu unless pressured to do so. I was not in a position to interview Zhu because my amicable relationship with Master Wei prevents any contact with Zhu, but popular sympathy in the Tianjin *quyi* community is clearly in favor of Wei. Most performers and consumers perceive Zhu Min as a stubborn and rebellious performer with ability but no sense of tradition. By severing her ties to Master Wei, Zhu has been stigmatized in the community as the student who was never good enough to follow in Wei's footsteps.

From Wei's point of view, not having a disciple is tragic—she has no successors and knows her genre will not survive after her death. The same kind of committee that convened to evaluate Master Jiang's career. and that urged Ji to become Jiang's official disciple in order to establish Jiang's artistic legitimacy, will also convene for Master Wei, but there will be no candidates for discipleship. As Ji explained to me, not having a disciple is a deficiency that will detract from her otherwise legendary status.

By the same token, however, the fact that all of Wei's former students have failed to emulate her implies that Wei's artistry is matchless. Neither her colleagues (*shimei*) nor her students have been able to imitate, let alone challenge, her singing style. Her superiority is unchallenged, making her relationship with any other performer in the genre like an *yitouchen* type of a Comic Routines performance. Perhaps Zhu sensed that Master Wei might not have wanted a disciple; this would explain Zhu's brazen behavior and establishment of her own style. From Wei's perspective, however, her unchallenged superiority will be a fragile victory recorded in the annals of *quyi* history, where the longevity of an artistic line is paramount.

Case Three: A disciple without a master

While lacking artistic progeny is tragic for a master performer, lacking a master can be equally devastating for a young singer. Bao, a singer who has tried to navigate a career without the help of a master, describes the beginning of her career as follows.

> In the early 1970s I was accepted to study quyi *at the Tianjin Municipal Narrative Arts Troupe along with four other students. I was 15 years old at the time. Each day we had to rise at 5:30 a.m. to* han sangzi *("shout out" or*

warm up our voices). After which, we practiced elocution by saying tongue twisters. At 6:00 we rested briefly, followed by physical exercise at 6:30, washing at 7:00, breakfast at 7:30, and class at 8:00. Each of us attended four 45-minute classes each morning, which amounted to studying four different genres at the same time. This was an opportunity for the Troupe to determine which genre would be the most suitable for each student. After lunch and a nap, we would either practice individually or listen to rehearsals or performances. Evenings were spent reading or studying. The only free time we had was from 4:00 p.m. Saturday afternoon, when we were allowed to go home, until Sunday morning at 9:00, when we were expected to return to the Troupe.

We spent three years in this very rigorous program. Of the five of us, the two male students in our group were not able to continue their vocal studies after their voices changed and have since become accompanists, and the two other female students were originally students of Master Wei but were also unable to continue after their voices had changed. While accompaniment was a ready option for the male students, the female students had no other recourse except to write off the three years of study at the troupe and find some other kind of work. Sometimes an unsuccessful vocal student may be allowed to work in some kind of related activity, such as archiving or research, but she rarely has options to perform as an accompanist since the main accompanying instruments are still played only by male performers. Of those original five students, I am the only one singing professionally today. With each group of new students that was accepted up through 1986 (when the Academy was established), the attrition rate has been similar.

After graduating from the troupe's training program, I was sent to Beijing to perform in front of a committee of specialists. Originally, one of my male classmates was earmarked as a candidate for my genre. Although a clear preference for female singers had emerged by this time, this genre had been sung in recent decades by both male and female performers, and the troupe felt that a male student might provide a welcome change to the female monopoly. When this young man was unable to continue to sing after his voice change, however, the committee in Beijing decided that I should study this genre. My voice was particularly well suited for the relatively low range that is characteristic of the style. I was not given a choice, but I was happy with the decision anyway.

I began studying pronunciation with Master Jiang. After a certain point, though, I wanted more specialized help for my particular genre. It was at that point that I decided to go to the Tianjin Broadcasting Station, where the archives had a large collection of audiotapes of the greatest performer of my genre who had passed away several decades before. Every morning at 8:00, I went to a small room at the radio station where I listened to and transcribed the lyrics of recordings made by this woman. In this way I not only learned many of the traditional pieces, but also learned the musical idiosyncrasies of the genre so that I was able to compose new pieces as well.

While Bao had been respected early in her career, she never won first place in any major competition. Invariably, the other young performers who had won awards had masters who were prominent in the community and supportive of the disciple's career. Consequently, Bao decided to approach Yu Xiaokai, one of the most respected *sanxian* players in the Troupe, and asked if he would be her *xianshi* (lead accompanist). Bao's natural ability, coupled with Yu's political influence, gave her a competitive edge that few of her classmates possessed. While Bao never formally became Yu's disciple (since it is no longer fashionable for an accompanist to accept disciples), she nonetheless reaped all the benefits that a disciple could expect from this relationship.[21] As a gifted composer, Yu arranged all her music, coached her singing, and became a boon to her career simply by virtue of his role as accompanist and mentor. Yu, on the other hand, enjoyed the financial and artistic benefits of being professionally associated with a talented singer. But Bao was ambivalent about the arrangement because her gains in artistic excellence were offset by the loss of her independence. Unlike a master, whose influence is felt primarily during the initial training period, a lead accompanist works with the singer on an ongoing basis for many years. Yu was a strict taskmaster and Bao felt indentured to him.[22]

In the early 1990s, Bao tried to break away from Yu in an attempt to establish her individuality as an artist. Finding herself incapable of furthering her career without his guidance, however, she reluctantly returned, and as a result, other performers spoke disparagingly of her dependent relationship. At this point in her career, Bao was considered a subordinate with no tactical or musical skills to challenge Yu's dominance.

Shortly after her return to Yu, however, Bao consented to an arrangement that surprised many people. In 1992, Bao and two other performers became the disciples of an elderly female performer named Master Jin, whose career was being evaluated by the troupe in the same way Jiang's had been several years previously. When it became apparent that Jin had no disciples, Bao and the two other performers were asked if they would consent to this relationship, even though Bao had never before studied with Jin.

For an established performer who had trained under the auspices of the Tianjin Municipal *Quyi* Arts Troupe to enter into this type of subordinate relationship may have appeared strange at the time, but it gave Bao the opportunity to break away from Yu. He would still function as her main accompanist (primarily for financial reasons), but he would also have to comply with Jin's wishes. On one level it might appear that Bao was simply trading one master for another. Functionally, however, their roles actually cancelled each other out: Bao has been able to take advantage of both Yu's musical abilities and Jin's standing in the community, yet she is no longer obliged to be bullied by Yu. Because Bao was already an established performer, Jin has not dared to control Bao's career. As a performer with multiple, mutually exclusive allegiances, Bao was able to use her *penggende*-like power to play her accompanist against her master, and was therefore able to minimize their authority over her as a subordinate. Bao's deliberate choices exemplified the most imaginative and successful manipulation of relationship strategies I witnessed in Tianjin.

Negotiating relationships in liminal space: The interdependence of masters and disciples

This study of a handful of female narrators in Tianjin is not intended as a representative statement about power relations among Chinese women or as a full-scale analysis of master–disciple relationships in modern Chinese performing arts. Indeed, this community of female performers is, in many ways, a cultural anomaly because of the historical circumstances that gave birth to the urban narrative tradition in Tianjin in the early twentieth century. Nonetheless, the relationships between female masters and disciples demonstrate two universal outcomes: An inevitable impasse when a disciple tries to assert her independence from her master, and a sophisticated use of *guanxi* tactics to mediate that impasse—tactics that are practiced by all members of Chinese society, male or female. The master's strategies involved acquiring disciples to gain status and establish her artistic lineage, and curtailing disciples' careers to keep potential rivalries in check. The disciple's strategies involved submitting initially to a master to gain skills and a network of professional relationships in order to establish her own power base, and eventually withholding support in order to assert power over her master.

The women of *quyi* have been able to skillfully negotiate their positions as superiors and subordinates within the context of master–disciple relationships. Master performers occupy *dougende*-like roles; however, in the same way that the *dougende* never has absolute power over the *penggende*, one cannot assume that female masters have absolute power over disciples. Master Jiang's career reveals her dependence upon her subordinates, thereby exposing her vulnerability. While Bao's career demonstrates the need for a subordinate to become part of an established network, she has been able to manipulate her subordinate position to her advantage.

Neither master nor disciple can function without recognizing the mutual interdependence of both roles. Sun Longji's comment about Chinese relationships is appropriate here: "In Chinese culture, the 'dyadic' relationship where 'there is a me inside of you; and there is a you inside of me' is something that approximates a 'cultural law.' It can be played out with many possibilities" (quoted in Yang 1989: 39). The master and disciple must continually adopt new strategies in order to re-create the relational space between them since there is an infinite number of ways to play out those relationships. Women are not merely victims of more powerful male or female colleagues. Since upward mobility is implied in the *penggende*-like subordinate position, when a female narrator assumes the role of a subordinate to either a male or female superior, there is a tacit expectation that she will try to improve her status professionally by making alliances with other performers. As a subordinate gradually improves her status, however, an intense rivalry often ensues. The gradual change from an *yitouchen*-type of relationship to a more competitive *zimugen*-type is common, especially when the young subordinate has everything to gain by trying to outdo her superior. Men in subordinate positions also practice this kind of strategy, but because women have become more accustomed to occupying positions of subordination in most situations, they have become particularly skilled at navigating a subordinate status (Wolf 1974: 164).

As women who learned how to thrive in the liminal areas of culture, female narrators in Tianjin became, unsurprisingly, especially adept at negotiating their roles as both masters and disciples. The examples of female narrators who successfully utilized the adaptive strategies implied by the roles in Comic Routines exhibited the same kind of expertise in liminal negotiation as they have demonstrated throughout this book—expertise in navigating the space between masculinity and femininity; text and tune; fantasy and reality; voice and body; and master and disciple. And their formidable abilities as liminal beings enabled them to communicate through the most important medium of all—the inimitable feminine voice.

Notes

1 I am translating *tudi* as disciple, instead of apprentice, to connote the intensity of the relationship between disciple and master teacher. In this context, I do not mean to imply any kind of spiritual association between *shifu* and *tudi* similar to the relationships between sages and their disciples.

2 Kristeva's notion of abjection (1982, 1987, 1989) is a rich theoretical discourse that I only mention superficially within the context of my argument about liminal relationships among women in the *quyi*. For a few selected secondary sources that explore some of the controversial aspects of Kristeva's ideas about abjection, see Oliver (1993), Nye (1987), Creed (2007), and Schippers (2011).

3 According to Margaret Wan, Hei Niu did replace Bai Niu after the latter performer left the stage.

4 See Gold, Guthrie, and Wank (2008) for a book-length study about the nature of *guanxi*, seen through the lens of social science research.

5 My need for a *baishihui* and Master Li's refusal to share information during our interview are examples of these two tactics (see Prologue).

6 *Xiangsheng*, which I have translated as Comic Routines, literally means "face and voice routines" (Link 1984: 83), and usually refers to the two-person form that is more precisely known as *duikou xiangsheng*. However, *xiangsheng* also includes two other varieties: *dankou xiangsheng*, or Comic Monologue (discussed briefly in Chapter 2), and *qunhuo xiangsheng*, which is a Comic Routine involving three or more actors (Tsau 1979–80: 54). All references in this chapter are to the two-person variety known as *duikou xiangsheng*.

7 Professor Xue's discussion of the roles in Comic Routines is supported by Moser's (1990) article on the piece known as *On Joke-Cracking and Joke-Setting (Lun Pengdou)*—a self-reflexive work in which the two comic actors taunt each other about the importance of their respective roles.

8 My research has reinforced what Robertson (1989: 225) has said regarding the study of music (and, by extension, the performing arts in general) as a "point

of entry for understanding how people achieve what they want within their own environment, how they act out their assumptions about each other, and how they challenge authority."

9 See Tsau (1979–80) and Moser (1990) for detailed explanations of these different roles.

10 Yang discusses the relational construction of people in a Chinese social context that supports the current description of social relationships as embodied by actors who perform Comic Routines (1989: 39). Lawson further discusses relational dynamics in social intercourse through the lens of Comic Routines (2011: 121–122).

11 See Stevens for a discussion of the potential antagonism between masters and disciples (1975: 60).

12 The account of my own discipleship in the Prologue is a case in point.

13 It turns out that audiences also support the students who mimic their masters exactly, and it is rare that a disciple will be good enough to convert audiences to her idiosyncrasies if her master is popular and well established. In most cases, if a disciple does challenge her master and tries to develop an independent style, the master will become increasingly uncomfortable and audiences will usually balk—unless the new style is undeniably good.

14 Although it would have been beneficial to interview Master Jiang, my friendship with Master Ji prevented me from ever having a relationship with Master Ji's antagonistic master.

15 This was the stringed instrument that accompanied Bai Niu's performance described in Chapter 2. For more information about the *sanxian*, see Stevens (1975: 142–144).

16 Refer to the Prologue for more information regarding the significance of the *baishihui*.

17 If she had not, she would have been considered an amateur performer in the old society.

18 Ji's refusal to respond to Jiang's request is a clear example of withholding support in order to curtail her master's professional development.

19 While Ji was considered a daughter at the time of her adoption, their relationship eventually developed as rival performers rather than as mother and daughter.

20 For a fascinating analysis of the power of the weaker agent in social relationships, see Yang's discussion of the principle of *guanxi* (1989: 45). For a more current discussion of *guanxi*, see Gold, Guthrie, and Wank (2008).

21 The fact that a *xianshi* (string master) no longer accepts disciples as he once might have done is significant. This illustrates the way in which female performers have carved out a niche for themselves as master teachers, supplanting one of the standard roles for string masters in pre-1949 Tianjin.

22 One interesting postscript to my interview with Bao was the following remark. After my own ceremony marking my discipleship to two performers in the community, Bao whispered to me, "Now those women cannot deny you anything you ask them for!"

Conclusion: Masters of Liminal Space

The overarching theme of this book is the acknowledgment of the considerable power of the female voice, which has been underscored by the unusual amount of energy used to keep female singers off public stages, often replacing them with androgynous male performers. In the changing political climate of Republican Tianjin, however, the power of androgyny associated with the male *dan* was transferred to the more politically suitable women of *quyi*. As a consequence, the women of *quyi* eventually became the preferred androgynous icons in Tianjin because they were able to simultaneously capitalize on their voices while minimizing their bodies in performance, thereby presenting a socially acceptable and politically advantageous solution to the voice and body problem.

Due to their status as icons of liminality, the women of *quyi* were unusually skilled at navigating the ambiguous areas of Chinese culture—the very places where the Chinese are wont to create art. By virtue of their roles as storytellers, they were mediums who conjured up stories, connecting their real-life audiences with imaginary worlds and transforming the ordinary into the extraordinary. As vocalists, they navigated the realm between word tone and melody, using music to elevate poetry and poetry to elevate music. As third-person narrators, they bridged the gap between male and female, creating an androgynous persona that enabled them to gain acceptance in a world that had been unwelcoming to female performers on public stages. As master performers, they became mentors for the young women who aspired to follow in their footsteps, despite the seemingly insurmountable challenges inherent in master-disciple relationships. In other words, they facilitated journeys between disparate cultural realms, making connections between music and life as they sang their way to respectability and social change.

The women of *quyi* began their ascent alongside the publication of Liu E's novel in 1907 and had declined in importance by the time Zhu Xueying's poem was published in 1985. When I first arrived in Tianjin (well after the heyday of urban *quyi* in that city), I found myself trying to understand a community whose halcyon days had passed—a world in which female narrators had once heroically made their mark several decades before—and studying Zhu's poem was one of the first steps in my quest to understand their story.

A story about a storyteller's voice, Zhu's narrative poem about Bai Niu is extraordinary for many reasons, not the least of which is its heroine's remarkable vocal talent, representing a metaphysical feminine trait. Descriptions of her voice are similar to descriptions of the voices of male *dan*, who were the first earthly incarnations of metaphysical femininity in late Qing and Republican Tianjin.[1] Elaborately yet modestly dressed female impersonators who sang in falsetto, the male *dan* literally embodied qualities of romanticized femininity by eliminating the female body problem and creating an otherworldly sound as they sang, and Bai Niu and her own ethereal voice and de-emphasized body may be seen as a literary depiction of female impersonation. As a consequence, the male *dan*, in an indirect way, and Bai Niu, in a more obvious way, became the inspiration for many of the women of *quyi*, who were able to appropriate metaphysical femininity for their benefit.

Zhu's poem is also about a performance that is best "heard" via auditory imagination through the act of reading. The reader of the poem is incapable of physically listening to the performance, but this does not matter. Early Chinese cosmology teaches that soundless sounds are more potent than audible sounds, and the description of her performance, including the references to "after tones," certainly implies those ancient aesthetic principles. For that reason, Bai's Niu's vocal talent is actually better appreciated through language than through listening—a situation that seems ironic only from a Western perspective. For this narrative poem, the one attempt at a vocal rendition by a female singer simply did not match up to the poetic description of Bai Niu.[2] Indeed, music's ability to "write" literature represents a highpoint of liminal play in this narrative piece.

The discussion about the liminal relationship between music and language does not end with the story about Bai Niu. Luo Yusheng's vocal rendition of "Listening to the Bells at Sword Pavilion" may be seen as a real-life complement to Bai Niu's fictional performance. Written by a disenfranchised Manchu writer who empathizes with his metaphysical heroine, the words of the poem seem to beg for a female singer to give voice to the wronged heroine; and in her masterful 1961 performance, Luo Yusheng breathes life into Lady Yang's tragic story. Since the emperor does not hear the deceased Lady Yang's ghostly voice or see her as an apparition in this version of the story, her abandonment becomes unbearable for him. Therefore, the living voice of a female narrator provides a musical fulfillment of and complement to the emperor's poetic expressions of searing loneliness, agony, and guilt over Lady Yang's death. Luo's legato singing style also compensates for the staccato nature of the poetry, filling in the linguistic gaps with melody and ornamentation in a way that perfectly balances the Chinese language. By providing a vocal realization of the lyrics and a space between verses through the instrumental interludes, Luo's performance fosters an alternate state of consciousness that permits the audience to contemplate the story differently than if they were simply to read the lyrics. In "Listening," then, Lady Yang's silence becomes a veritable invitation for a female voice—a situation in which the literary poem "writes" the musical rendition. And Luo's audible voice for the deceased metaphysical heroine provides a counterpart to Lao Can's poetic description of Bai Niu's fictive voice.

Given the centuries of female silence on Chinese public stages, the ability of Luo Yusheng and other female narrators to give voice to metaphysical heroines was a heroic feat in itself. As the "corporeal resonance of the female body—the purely sonorous, bodily element of the vocal utterance" (Dunn and Jones 2001: 2), the sound of the female voice was inevitably linked to the female body problem. Until the social changes initiated in the Republican period, reputable women did not even appear on stage, and even then, female performers were often consumed voyeuristically, preventing them from pursuing their craft like their male counterparts. The women of *quyi*, however, were able to occupy a unique space. By highlighting the feminine through their voices, de-emphasizing their bodies, and assuming an androgynous persona as third-person narrators, the women of *quyi* were able to take full advantage of metaphysical femininity.

Although the reasons for the historical significance of female icons were probably unknown to the women of *quyi*, female narrators were nonetheless attracted to heroines who had already engendered sympathy and respect for female impersonators and for well-educated male writers who used feminine icons in their writings. Accordingly, in their unique androgynous position, the women of *quyi* took advantage of appropriating existing powerful stories about tragic victims whose stories were, in many cases, similar to their own.[3] Drawing upon audience sympathy for their metaphysical heroines, female narrators were able to transfer that sympathy to themselves through the commutability implied by culturally ubiquitous *qi*. In the same way that male writers and male *dan* were able to benefit from the transferability of positive womanly qualities from their heroines, the women of *quyi* were empowered by being associated with metaphysical heroines through the act of performance.

In addition to profiting from the metaphysical femininity that was deeply ingrained in Chinese culture, the women of *quyi* were also able to rise above the underclass into which they were born because progressively minded political leaders emphasized gender equity as China sought to enter the modern world. The congruence of unfortunate lowborn women singing texts about female victims was significant in creating a culturally acceptable employment opportunity for poor women in the Republic at a time when international feminism had made important inroads among forward-thinking intellectuals and leaders. Subsequently, singing stories about metaphysical heroines became one of the means by which the women of *quyi* were able to translate the image of beleaguered heroines into a performance persona that captivated audiences and eventually assured female performers a secure niche in a political climate that was increasingly anxious for more female participation. Taking advantage of time-honored stories and the changing political thinking of the time, the women of *quyi* simultaneously became traditors, as they continued existing cultural practices, and pioneers, as they pursued new paths for self-expression and financial independence.

Through the act of singing the stories and revealing a shrewd entrepreneurial spirit—not unlike the tactical intelligence displayed by the heroine in "Melted Candlesticks"—the women of *quyi* were able to succeed in a modernizing China. As female performers established themselves in respectable careers, they began to contemplate their legacy as vocal artists. Intrinsic to Chinese culture is the need for progeny, and the women of *quyi* were eventually encouraged to solicit female disciples in order to establish their artistic lines. Although the notion of females soliciting female disciples is unusual, Republican Chinese culture encouraged the practice, and female narrators negotiated the space between masters and disciples similar to the way the *dougende* and *penggende* actors interact in Comic Routines. Whether in the superior or subordinate position, female narrators became proficient at navigating the secondary abjection inherent in the system and tailoring it to carry on their uniquely female art form.

While the story of the singers who followed in the footsteps of Bai Niu is fascinating, it is also idiosyncratic. The impact of the women of *quyi* in contemporary Chinese culture is minimal, but their legacy is inspiring. By embracing the ambiguity and uncertainty of liminal space available to all culture bearers, the women of *quyi* took advantage of a rich traditional culture—replete with heroic stories about women and a time-honored tradition of androgynous performance—and used their newfound political freedom to perform those stories in their own voices. As one of many figurative voices in the complex cultural counterpoint of female experiences in Republican Tianjin, the story of the women of *quyi* is a stunning theme in the larger, overarching study of Chinese women.

The idiosyncratic female storytellers communicated messages of universal importance for all modern Chinese. In discussing the way that poetry creates a discourse for Bedouin women, Abu-Lughod explains that "the communication of sentiment in poetry allows individuals to frame their experience as similar to those of others and perhaps to assert the universality of their experiences" (1999: 239). Similarly, by singing stories about inspiring heroines, the women of *quyi* both sang about feminine role models who represented the best of Chinese culture and exemplified ways in which all Chinese can become successful, respected, and socially mobile, thereby becoming universally inspiring icons themselves.

Postscript

An example of the ongoing influence of the women of *quyi* is a fairly recently aired 38-minute documentary about Luo Yusheng.[4] Broadcasted in 2012, ten years after her death, the documentary was designed both to remind an older audience of and introduce a younger audience to Luo's role as one of the performers recorded in the production of *Four Generations Under One*

Roof (*Sishitongtang*), a famous television series based on a novel by Lao She that first aired in 1984. The documentary begins as the producers of *Four Generations* discuss the need for a singer for the theme song—a singer whose style would reflect Beijing culture during the era of Japanese occupation. They decided upon Luo Yusheng. When the producers first asked Luo to sing the theme song, she was already 71 years old, retired, and reticent to take on the challenge. Undeterred, the producers pressed her to find out why she was unwilling. She admitted that she was not a singer in the traditional sense, and she certainly could not sing in the pop music style of the mid-1980s. But the reason for her refusal was precisely the reason they wanted her voice; establishing authenticity in their production required a voice that would be appropriate to the historical context of the work, and given her background and contribution to the narrative forms so popular at the time, Luo was the clearly best choice for the part.

Although she had recorded her voice many times throughout her life, she had not worked with as many musicians—particularly those trained in Western music—as she did on this project. With a small Western-style orchestra to supplement the traditional instruments, she felt somewhat intimidated at first, but rose to the occasion. When the other musicians and actors first heard her in rehearsal, they were dumbfounded by her deep, resonant sound and her exceptionally large range as her voice echoed through the studio. The other performers on the set were also amazed at her memory. She was able to memorize texts more quickly than the younger singers and actors despite the fact that she was decades older than most of them.

Given Luo's extraordinary voice, quick wit, and memory, it became clear that she was a force to be reckoned with, and eventually the producers realized that her own story needed to be told. While Luo was a legend among members of the local and national *quyi* communities, she was not necessarily recognized as a national figure when she first performed on the set of *Four Generations* in 1984. In order to remedy this oversight, Luo was interviewed about her life and long performance career, and photographs and short video clips from her legendary 1961 performance of "Listening to the Bells at Sword Pavilion" were included in the footage, allowing audiences to hear her at the peak of her talent. It was as though Bai Niu had finally appeared in human form—and on television at that—one hundred years after her first appearance in Lui's novel.

An anachronism in 1984, Luo Yusheng was nonetheless able to command a small following among those who learned about her art form. In 2012, when the documentary was aired on the tenth anniversary of her death, larger audiences became aware of her unusual life and contributions to twentieth-century Chinese culture. While she may have been the greatest example of a modern Bai Niu, she was certainly not the only one. The stories and songs of the two dozen or so women of *quyi* constitute a small but impressive contribution to the global study of the female voice—with all of its cultural implications and in all of its varied manifestations.

Notes

1 Interestingly, Lao Can is the intermediary who brings Bai Niu's metaphysical performance to life through his poetic narrative in the same way the male *dan* realizes
 a metaphysical heroine through his theatrical performance.
2 See n5 in Chapter 2.
3 See the two case studies in Chapter 1.
4 See Zhao (2012), and Chapter 3 n16.

Epilogue

Often alienated by the perceived reductionism of science, many musicologists are unconvinced about the relevance of biological perspectives regarding the origins of music. Should ethnomusicologists and music historians even consider such questions? Given that most musicologists have not addressed reasons as to why the female voice has inspired both fascination and ambivalence, I dare to wonder. Some scholars from a variety of different scientific fields suggest that human music and language may have a feminine origin—a fact that might explain the strong androcentric resistance to the power and significance of the female voice in many music cultures throughout history. While the research is clearly speculative at this point, I have found it provocative nonetheless, and share some of the highlights below.

In the compendium *Communicative Musicality: Exploring the Basis of Human Companionship* (Oxford 2010), editors Malloch and Trevarthen argue persuasively that "communicative musicality" (hereafter CM)—the interactions between mothers and their pre-linguistic infants—follows rules of musical performance, demonstrating that this gentle form of communication is the "essential foundation for all forms of communication, even the most refined and technically elaborated" (2010: back cover). Noted psychoanalyst and language theorist Julia Kristeva also discusses a symbiotic relationship between mothers and pre-linguistic infants, which represents what she terms the "semiotic" phase (1984: 25–27). During the semiotic phase, the child communicates in "gurgling and babbling noises ... that resemble a musical, rhythmic sound and that lack sense, meaning and structure" (Schippers 2011: 26). Whereas Kristeva's analysis of this pre-Oedipal communication between mother and infant implies a lack of rules and order, scholars who espouse the notion of CM disagree. Malloch and Trevarthen explain:

> With the help of gifted young collaborators entranced by the opportunity to make discoveries starting from the simple premise that mother–infant play is intelligent and creative, in Edinburgh Colwyn traced the growth of infants' motives for sharing intentions and feelings in human

company ... All the while, whether in Scotland, Nigeria, Germany, Sweden, or Japan, researchers found that mothers spoke to infants with similar rhythms and intonation, and infants moved in sympathy

(2009: 2).

As a consequence, the exaggerated prosody and bodily gestures characteristic of the way mothers speak to their infants appear to be universal and, significantly, the infants themselves actively solicit CM.[1]

Ethologist Ellen Dissanayake, one of the contributors to the compendium, argues that communicative musicality is also biologically adaptive, meaning that CM developed because it solved problems of survival and reproduction in human evolution (2010: 20–24). Unlike Geoffrey Miller's adaptationist theory, which considers the origin of music to have emerged from a male competitive display for females (2000: 338–344), Dissanayake claims that

> by treating all products of the human brain as a form of sexual signaling, Miller ... offers no cognitive function that is primary to music ... no need that is fulfilled by its specific character that is not equally fulfilled by any other skill or display behaviour.
>
> (2010: 21)

Dissanayake also feels that Miller's sexual selection argument does not address the cooperative uses of music, which is a primary consideration for her and other scholars,[2] and believes that one of the strengths of the argument in favor of CM as a biological adaptation lies in the way it solves both evolutionary problems by promoting maternal reproductive success and ensuring the survival of the infant. Dissanayake states:

> A bipedal stance requires changes in bones and muscles that were originally used for quadrupedal locomotion. Among these alterations is a narrowed pelvis, making for difficulties at parturition for both the mother and her large-brained infant—a trend that was well underway by 1.6 million years ago ... The solution (or compromise) was that selection favoured infants who were born at an increasingly premature state. Over evolutionary time, hominid babies gradually became much more helpless at birth than those of other primates
>
> (2010: 22).

The resultant longer periods of infant altriciality necessitated effective communication between hominid mothers and their underdeveloped babies. As a consequence, the affiliative vocalizations, body movements, and facial expressions characteristic of communicative musicality, enhanced by the release of hormones after birth, were essential for promoting emotional conjoinment between mother and infant and for enhancing cognitive and social skills for infants (22). Dissanayake continues:

It appears ... that hominid mothers of helpless, demanding offspring required additional insurance to guarantee that they would willingly devote constant attention and care to them for years. How else to explain why shortly after birth (and at least as early as four weeks), human mothers and infants universally engage in dyadic species-specific interactions that serve to coordinate their behaviour and emotions—what Malloch and Trevarthen call "communicative musicality"? (22)

Cross and Morley also argue that the vocalizations between infants and caregivers likely had an adaptive value: "Music can be interpreted as one of those [adaptive] mechanisms, emerging under the selection pressures of the progressive extension and stage-differentiation of the juvenile period in the later hominid lineage" (2010:74). These proto-musical and proto-linguistic vocalizations may have been the precursor of human language as well as music. Dissanayake makes similar claims about the role of mother–infant communication as a precursor to human music (2010: 20–23).[3] Mithen, whose argument predates the research published in *Communicative Musicality*, also believes that the dyadic communication between mothers and infants is reminiscent of an ancient protolanguage that existed early in the hominid line— one that diverged into what we know today as music and language in modern humans (2006: 276).

Not all scholars subscribe to the notion that CM is an adaptive trait that has evolved into music, and other adaptationist theories concerning reproduction or survival benefits abound (Thompson 2009: 21–32). Some scholars propose that music is an "exaptation"—a trait that performs a completely different function from the one for which it evolved (33). Others suggest that nonadaptationist mechanisms led to the evolution of music, arguing that music is a technological spin-off of other cognitive processes, and is not biologically necessary. Some scholars who espouse nonadaptationist theories recognize that the different components of music may have had different origins (Thompson 33–34). Steven Pinker famously stated that activating certain auditory processes produces pleasures not unlike eating cheesecake (2009: 528), and suggests that music is comparable to ingesting recreational drugs.

To date, scholars working in the sciences have dominated the conversation regarding the origin of music. Paul Armstrong's groundbreaking work *How Literature Plays with the Brain: The Neuroscience of Reading and Art*, addresses the problems associated with the disciplinary divide between the humanities and sciences. Referring to some of the neuroscientific and phenomenological research about the way the brain "plays" with literature, Armstrong, a professor of English, demonstrates how the fields of neuroscience and literary studies can be mutually beneficial. Armstrong explains some of the reasons why scientists and humanists seem unable to discuss areas of common interest, suggesting that scientists (neuroscientists in this case, but I believe his observations extend to scholars in other areas of scientific inquiry) frequently falter when they tackle aesthetic questions:

[Scientists] need guidance about aesthetics and literary theory from humanists, who have wider and deeper knowledge about these issues. What humanists have most to offer neuroscience comes from our long engagement with core questions having to do with the creation and interpretation of works of art—the great variety of artistic forms that occur across different historical periods and cultural traditions, the range of aesthetic experiences to which these can give rise ... and the widely differing, often conflicting theories that have been developed for this multiplicity

(Armstrong 2013: 181).

As a music scholar, I believe that most researchers who study the biological foundations of music lack a thorough understanding of the variety of musical expression across cultures and throughout history. CM is compelling to me because it coheres most clearly with the evidence I have uncovered in my research about female singers, and persuasively suggests a feminine origin for music, highlighting the significance of female voices and bodily gestures in the evolution of music and language. Moreover, the ubiquitous presence of CM with the birth of every child provides ongoing evidence of our ethological origins echoing through evolutionary time.

Recent research in the field of CM suggests the centrality of the female voice and body in communicating essential proto-musical and proto-linguistic information to infants—a process that is replicated in the master–disciple relationship. However, this book has been more concerned about what happens to the female voice *outside* of the mother–infant relationship. The way that the female voice is heard on public stages is a kind of co-opting of CM—an instance of appropriating the powerful female voice in the context of public performance, where it engenders a highly anxious response among male members of the audience, revealing a deeply rooted antagonism between the sexes because of the intrinsic evolutionary importance of female vocality.

Historically, the solution to dealing with the anxiety-producing female voice and body has been the containment of female singers in public performance and the replacement of conventional female singers with androgynous vocalists. In the case of the latter, boy trebles, castrati, and male *dan* provided popular substitutions for female singers, preserving the treble voice in a less anxiety-producing body. Male audience members are permitted to appreciate a kind of feminine vocality without the body problem, and female audience members can appreciate both the artistry and the sexual allure of an unintimidating, feminized male. By contrast, the direction of androgyny from female to male normally implies insubordination, unless androgynous women, like the women of *quyi*, showcased the female voice in a de-emphasized female body. In the case of the women of *quyi*, the female narrators not only provided a less anxiety-producing solution to the female voice and body problem than conventional female singers, but also served the aims of the

Chinese state by promoting a masculinized, empowered femininity that was nonetheless dictated and delimited by the government narrative aimed at the masculine endeavor of nation building.

All of these solutions to the female voice and body problem are rooted in an androcentric fear of the evolutionarily powerful female voice. But I would also argue that female audience members respond to androgynous male singers in a way that suggests a strong erotic attraction. It is possible that the treble voice in a male body is a form of sexual signaling aimed at female audience members—as well as an anxiety-reducing strategy designed for male attendees. Androgynous male singers may co-opt the treble voice to attract female fans to validate the importance of the primordial power of the female voice by making it a medium for sexual signaling. Females who portray male characters (like the female *sheng* and the *otokoyaku*) can attract some female audiences for the same reason that female fans seem to love androgynous men as approachable, non-threatening males. And androgynous female storytellers who sing with a treble voice can be the one type of singer whose sexuality is minimized enough for all audiences so that artistry can prevail. These outlooks represent a rich source for future research on the female voice and body in public settings.

Notes

1 See Mithen (2006: 72) and Dissanayake (2010: 23) for a brief discussion about the ways infants encourage this communication.
2 For example, ethnomusicologist John Blacking claims that cooperation in music is far and above one of the most noticeable qualities in the world's musical cultures (Blacking 1995: 31).
3 For a more extensive discussion about the adaptive value of mother–infant communication compared to some other theories about the origin of music, see Dissanayake (2000) and (2010: 18–26).

Appendices

Appendix 1

Chinese text for "Bai Niu Tells a Story"

白妞说书

朱 学 颖

I.

  1. 妙曲清音何处寻?
        大明湖畔觅芳尘.

  2. 《老残游记》传神韵,
        玉人绝调果超群。

  3. 书坛上,古来多少高明客
        谁如那白妞雅韵震曲林,
        真是声传九天外,情动万人魂。

II.

  4. 那济南的明湖居是说书的场地,
        在门前,有一纸招帖墨迹新。

  5. 上写着"白妞说书"四个字,
        引来了顾曲的周郎大驾临。

  6. 有一位江湖的郎中也来光顾,
        人称老残年近五旬。

  7. 他来到济南府不过才三、两日,
        有一事,心中不解起疑云:

  8. 在巷尾街头茶楼酒肆,
        道旁路侧水畔湖滨,

  9. 都夸白妞书说得好,
        万人一辞众口同音。

10. 真奇怪,说唱鼓书有什么妙处,
        却为何全城若狂落魄失魂?

11. 因此上，老残来到说书场，
    他要看一看，这白妞到底是怎样的人。

III.

12. 进得书场天尚早，
    离午后开书还有一个时辰。

13. 看了看，远近前后人都坐满，
    想要是找个落脚的地方都无处寻。

14. 无奈何，递给看座儿的钱一把，
    才在这板凳边儿上把座儿勾。

15. 园子里，人声嘈杂闲谈论，
    无非是那前朝的旧话，当世的新闻。

16. 书座儿中，有店铺的商人、文苑的名士，
    也有那府衙的官吏、市井的平民。

17. 老残他盼等多时心烦躁，
    好容易，从后台才走上来那唱曲儿的人。

18. 原来是天真无邪的一位少女，
    她在那弦鼓声中吐清音。

19. 唱一曲 声声宛转字字清脆，
    如黄莺出谷乳燕归林。

20. 最难得，一人演出一台戏，
    褒贬忠奸论古今，生旦净末细细地分，
    情深意态儿真，她的演唱才这么传神。

IV.

21. 这时候，少女下场人声又起，
    闹哄哄更比来时乱十分。

22. 说声、笑声、叫卖，声声不断，
    听邻桌上，正议论刚才唱曲儿的人。

23. 一个说："这姑娘唱得可真叫好，
    想来必是白妞本人？"

24. 另一个哈哈大笑连连摆手，
    说出话来儒雅斯文：

25. "她非是白妞乃黑妞是也，
    老兄你真是耳目不明黑白不分。

26. 这黑妞所学都是白妞的传授，
    那白妞的技艺，黑妞才学得了一、二分。

27. 黑妞的妙处能说能讲，
    白妞的妙处难觅难寻。

28. 一句话，不能言传只能意会，
    辨高下，你听后方知此话真。"

29. 说到这里话儿收住：
    "你休再问，快看白妞演书文。"

30. 老残他只觉得眼前一亮，
    顿时间，满台生辉全场生春。

31. 但见白妞款步出场，.
    明眸一闪，万声俱静鸦雀无音。

32. 座下客似待命的士卒听兵主调遣，
    那台上的白妞正是巾帼将军。

33. 老残他暗暗称奇唯自问：
    这情景，我几曾见来几曾闻？

34. 细看白妞才十八、九岁，
    穿一身淡雅无华的素衣裙，

35. 既没有脂粉气不俗不媚，
    又没有江湖气不厌不贫。

36. 论神采，似出水的莲花，临风的杨柳；
    看清姿，如新升的星座，乍涌的冰轮。

37. 此时节，全场肃然听白妞唱曲儿，
    一个个，凝视着书台上，都屏住了心神，举座尽知音。

V.

38. 见白妞，鼓板轻敲音清越，
    真能够怡神易性悦耳赏心。

39. 叮当当，两片铜简谐六律，
    韵悠悠，一面羯鼓定五音。

40. 但听得 弦索声微音袅袅，
    白妞她才眉扬目转启朱唇。

41. 一句一串珍珠落，
    石破天惊声韵夺人。

42. 果真是歌喉清润无瑕玉，
    洗尽泥沙荡俗尘。

43. 唱腔儿，裁云断锦新且巧；
    曲词儿，雅俗共赏浅又深；

44. 节拍儿，忽急忽缓皆如意；
    音调儿，或高或低尽随心。

45. 悲壮时，冻云冷雪山川恸，
    欢快时，暖日和风草木春；

46. 明丽时，江南景色清幽娟秀，
    遒劲时，大漠风光壮阔雄浑。

47. 书台下，数百听客呆呆坐，
    全忘了吸烟续水把茶斟，

48. 怕搅扰清音谁敢喝彩，
    这无形的禁令哪个不遵。

49. 老残他聆听妙曲如饮醇酒，
    恍惚惚，不知身何处，更难辨假真。

50. 只觉得眼前的景物全都变啦，
    唯有那白妞的声音耳内闻。

51. 这声音在前如磁石吸铁，
    老残他缓步而行随后跟。

52. 一处处，别有洞天如仙境，
    观不尽青山绿水空谷幽林。

53. 见四周：山泉清澈峰峦秀，
    松柏苍翠草如茵。

54. 花簇簇．叶蓁蓁，香馥馥，碧森森，
    百鸟落枝头，蜂蝶绕花荫，
    真乃是云蒸霞蔚五彩缤纷。

55. 忽听得，声腔儿一转拔地起，
    直上九霄逐风云。

56. 几次翻高节节险，
    凌空而下步步沉。

57. 谁说是"山重水复疑无路"，
    君不见"柳岸花明又一村"。

58. 但愿得俚曲传唱千秋远，
    长伴湖山万世存。

59. 猛然间，音断声歇收清韵，
    老残他如梦方醒稳住心神。

60. 却原来台上曲终人已去，
    空留下台下的座客醉沉沉。

61. 虽有这喝彩之声如雷震，
怎敌那白妞的余音漫乾坤。

62. 暗赞叹："此曲只应天上有，
人间能得几回闻?"

63. 大明湖，山光水色留余韵，
白妞她，金声玉振艺绝伦，风靡了多少听书顾曲的人。

Appendix 2
Chinese text for "Melted Candlesticks"

化蜡扦儿

这是我们街坊的一档子事——凡是这个特别的事都是我们街坊的！那位说："你在哪儿住哇？"这您别问，我就这么说，您就这么听，"姑妄言之，姑妄听之"。

这是前四十来年的事，我这家儿街坊是财主哇，富裕！站着房，躺着地，银行存着多少多少款。姓什么呢？姓狠。百家姓儿没有这个姓啊？顶好，没有顶好，回头遇见有同姓的他听着别扭！姓狠，这家子老夫妻俩，跟前仨儿子，一个姑娘。这仨儿子哪，是狠大、狠二、狠三啦！还有狠老头儿、狠老婆儿、狠老姑儿，这一家子狠到一块儿啦！这仨儿子都娶了媳妇啦，老姑儿哪？出阁啦。老姑儿出阁的时候儿，正赶上她们家那阵儿轰轰烈烈呀，聘这个老姑娘净嫁妆就六十四抬，樟木箱子八个，手使的家伙就够两堂。手使的家伙是什么呀？旧社会就讲究这个，茶壶、茶碗、撢瓶、帽筒，直顶到各式各样的磁器，完全是官窑定烧的。还有一套锡器，锡器是什么呀？茶叶罐啦，油灯啦，蜡扦子啦！油灯里头搁点儿蜜，洞房里点这个，"蜜里调油"嘛！净锡器就四十多斤，讲究！完完全全都是真正道口锡呀！什么叫道口锡呀？您要买锡家伙，你把它倒过来瞧，在底儿上有一个长方戳子印儿，是"点铜"两字，那是道口锡，您这么一弹哪，当当……铜声儿！打聘姑娘之后哇，没有二年吧，老头儿死啦，老头儿一死呀，剩个老婆儿啦，这老婆儿从这儿起就受苦啦！怎么受苦啦？老头儿一死谁当家哪？仨儿子全抢着当家！这妯娌仨不投缘，厨房的火一年到头老关着！因为什么？做饭做不完。大爷早晨想吃捞面，二爷呢，要吃烙饼，不在一块儿吃，三爷呀要吃贴饽饽熬鱼，大奶奶要吃干饭，二奶奶就吃花卷儿，三奶奶要吃馄饨，这可怎么弄！吃完了饭哪，都坐在屋里骂大街，有孩子骂孩子，没孩子骂猫，吵得街坊四邻不安哪！一宿一宿地吵。原先街坊给劝，后来连架都不给劝啦！怎么办哪？过不到一块儿，分家。

这一分家呀，把亲友都请来了，这叫吃散伙面。分家怎么分哪？一人分几处房子，房子有值多值少的，少的这个怎么办哪？少的这个拿银行里的钱往上贴补，银行里剩下的钱再分三份儿，屋里的家具分三份儿，直顶到剩一根儿筷子也剁三节儿！煤球儿数一数数儿！分来分去剩一个铜子儿，这一个子儿归谁？归谁都不成！怎么办啊？买一个子儿铁蚕豆分开，一人分几个，剩一个，剩一个扔到大街上，谁也别要！连鸡、猫、狗都分；可就是这个——妈妈怎么办哪！跟谁过啊？没人管，没想到那儿！分了家呀，大爷还住这个老宅子，二爷、三爷呀搬出去。都分完了，门口儿拴大车往外装东西，二爷、三爷不等亲友走他们就走。

"众位亲友，我们先走一步，我们得拾掇拾掇去，新安家呀！"

他们这位老姑娘啊，别瞧这是女的，年纪不大，三十挂点儿零，嗬！心里有算计啊！打来到这儿，就笑呵呵地坐着，什么话也没说，等到这个时候儿才说话："二哥、三哥就这么走吗？"

"老妹子，你这儿坐着吧，我们不等吃晚饭啦，我们得去安置安置。"

"别忙啊，这儿还有没分完的你们就走吗？"

哥儿仨都愣啦，不知道还有什么东西没分完。

"哎哟，想不到啦，老妹子帮忙吧，你提个醒儿，还有什么？"

"这儿还有个妈呀！这妈是怎么分哪？你们是把她勒死了分三份儿是怎么着？还是活着剁呀？"

"那谁敢哪！"

亲友们都在这儿，听着这话有劲！老太太养活闺女没白养活，好！这哥儿仨半天没说出话来。大爷领头儿："对，对，老妹妹这话对。勒死谁敢哪？应当啊分四份儿，有妈妈一份儿养老金，可是妈妈有个百年之后，剩多剩少不是还得由我们哥儿仨再分吗？那不费事了嘛！　今天一分就分完啦，省得费二回事。这个哪……妈妈怎么活着……这个有办法，一个月三十天哪，妈妈轮流住，今天不是初一吗？妈妈就在这儿，到十一呀二爷接，到二爷那儿去，二十一呀三爷接，到初一呀我再接回来。要送哪，逢十的日子晚上送，要送全送，要接全接。这怎么样？"

亲友们一听，这样儿成啦。"就这么办吧！"

大家各回各家。

头一天什么事没有，头天老太太晌午吃的散伙面，晚上吃的折罗。第二天早晨哪，老太太得吃大爷的饭啦！得，老太太从这儿起就受罪了！您瞧那意思可真好。老太太起来坐在那儿，儿媳妇——大奶奶给倒碗茶，儿子在旁边儿一站。

"小子你坐下。"

"我不用坐下，我不用坐下，您这是疼我呀，可是跟您一块儿坐着，亲友来了一瞧不老好看的，不说我不恭敬啊，哈哈，说您没有家规。……我有点儿事情跟您商量，您今天要是喜欢呢我就说，您要是不喜欢呢，这两天说也成。"

老太太说："什么事呀？你说。"

"您喜欢吗？"

"我有什么不喜欢的，说吧！"

"是，您让我说我就说，嗯——您愿意我露脸哪？您愿意我要饭哪？"

老太太说："这是什么话呀？十个手指头咬哪个都疼啊，我愿意你们全露脸哪！我干什么愿意你们要饭！"

"是，是，您疼我呀，我知道，您也愿意我露脸，我也愿意我露脸，无奈一节呀，这个脸不好露。在一块儿过呀，不洒汤不漏水，他们哥儿俩都比我有能耐；那么分了家了哪，这就得八仙过海各显其能。他们都有事由儿，我可就这点儿死水儿，怎么办哪？我就得口里省肚里攒，牙齿缝里往下刮，吃点儿不好的，吃点儿棒子面儿什么的！为什么跟您说这话？怕您难受哇！一个月您在这儿才住十天，这十天之内呀，您想吃什么给您做，给您做呀可就够您一人儿吃的，您可别给孩子他们分，我们吃半顿呀您也别管，我们喝粥啊，饿一顿呀，您也别难受，单给您做，您想吃什么呀回头您吩咐。"

老太太说："这个不像话，不对不对，不对！干吗给我单做呀？你赶明儿个过好了还好！你有亏空了——让妈妈把你吃穷了！我可不落那个，我吃也吃不了多少，随随便便吧！一个月住十天哪，你做什么我吃什么，我最爱吃棒子面儿。"

"是，是，您最爱吃棒子面儿哪，就做您最爱吃的，您喜欢吃什么就给您做什么。大奶奶，做饭去！"

缺大德啦！他把这句话打老婆儿嘴里挤出来啦。大奶奶做饭去啦——棒子面儿，你蒸点儿窝头也好哇！窝头还软和，她贴饽饽！特意地多搁柴火，贴出来这么大个儿，这煳嘎渣儿倒有一半儿，连咸菜都没有！这老太太没有对口牙，她咬不动煳嘎渣儿呀，只好把它揭下来，啃那半儿软和的，吃了三分之一，这多半个贴饽饽就吃不下去啦！馋？不是，人一到五十往外呀差不多都有这现象，"非肉不饱"，嘴里咽不下去啦，肚子可饿。怎么着哪？就算饱啦！把这饽饽搁这么啦，心想：没饱哇，没饱不要紧哪，等晚上吧，晚饭他不得做点儿面汤吗？拿面汤泡饽饽也能吃呀！想错啦，晚上不用做饭啦，有饽饽哪！凉了，凉了给老太太烤烤哇！这一烤不更吃不动了吗？

他们这一家子可也吃，弄块饽饽头哇在老太太跟前举着，好歹咬两口就搁在笸箩里，不吃啦，饱啦！大爷呀带着俩大小子出去玩儿去啦，应名儿玩儿去，在外头不管哪个饭馆儿随便吃点儿嘛儿，吃完再回来！大奶奶哪？抱着小的带着姑娘上街坊家串门儿斗十胡去啦！饿了哪？掏出钱来让她们姑娘去买呀！大饼、酱肉啊足吃，吃完了再回来！核着这饽饽就给这老婆儿留着！打初二就吃起，直吃到初六，瞭了瞭这饽饽还有多一半儿！老太太一想：瞧这意思到初十也吃不了哇！上二爷那儿去吧！上二爷那儿去啦。临出门儿，儿子，儿媳妇都没问问上哪儿去，老太太也没提。

老太太到了二爷的家。一进二爷那个门儿，您瞧她那二儿子："妈，来啦！不是到十一你才来哪吗？怎么今天就来啦，是在我这儿住半个月是怎么着？为什么那天不把这话说明白了哇？"

老太太坐在那儿直喘："唉！你大哥呀贴了一锅饽饽，吃了五天还没吃了。我肚子饿，吃不下去！"

"就这么着嘛！就这么着嘛！他倒有贴饽饽呀，我们连贴饽饽都没有！您到了这儿反正我们得给您吃呀，能让您饿着吗？贴饽饽挺好您不吃，我们想吃还弄不着哪！哎，给您做点儿软和的吧，给您熬粥。"

买棒子面儿呀熬了一锅粥，这倒好，省牙啦！那边儿吃完喽贴饽饽，这儿拿粥一溜缝儿！半斤棒子面儿熬了一大锅，老太太喝了两天，一瞧，还有半锅哪！饿得眼前发黑，上三的那儿去吧！

一进三的门儿，她那三儿子就说："嗬！我说你怎么还不死呀？你死了不就完了吗！你死了，我们弄个白大褂儿一穿不就得了嘛！你这不是吃累人嘛！到二十一才是我的份儿，今天才几儿呀？还不到初十哪，这不是挤对人吗？"

老太太说："你大哥呀贴了一锅饽饽，我吃了五天，二哥那儿熬粥，喝了两天，还有一半儿，我肚子空啊，不饱！"

"就这么着嘛！他们有钱，他们不给你花，他们都抖起来啦，良心哪！你别瞧我分家的时候儿分钱分产业，都还了帐啦，短人家的不还那成吗？人家起诉！这房啊，这房都使了钱啦，典三卖四！打昨儿我们就没揭锅！您来啦，我们能让您饿着吗？我们去要饭不也得给您吃吗？妈妈嘛！我是没钱，哎，三奶奶有钱吗？"

"我哪儿有钱哪？我没有钱！"

"问问，哪个孩子身上有钱？"

问了半天，那大孩子腰里还有一个铜子儿。

"一个铜子儿买什么？得啦，给奶奶买一个子儿铁蚕豆。"

好哇！吃完了贴饽饽，弄点儿粥一溜缝儿，再弄几个铁蚕豆一磨牙！一天吃了仨，到晚上要睡觉啦，嘴里含了一个，睡着了差点儿噎死！老太太这么一想：就剩一个道儿，还有一个老姑娘，要是再不成啊，干脆跳河，没有别的法子！

出三爷门儿上老姑娘那儿去，走是走不了啊！没有劲啦，雇车。坐车到老姑娘门口儿下不了车——腰里没钱，告诉拉车的去叫门，叫她们小孩儿的小名儿，就说姥姥来啦！拉车的一叫门，老姑娘出来啦，一瞧妈妈这个样儿，抬头纹也开啦，耳朵梢儿也干啦，下巴颏儿也抖啦，七窍也塌啦，要死！瞧见老姑娘啊就要哭！这位姑奶奶够明白的，一边儿给老太太擦眼泪呀，一边儿掏车钱。

"别哭哇，别哭哇，让人笑话，屋里说去。"连拉车的帮着，把老太太搀进屋来，往那儿一坐。拉车的走啦，老太太还要说，叫闺女把嘴给捂住了："你别说啦，让人家街坊听见多笑话呀！你的心事我全知道，你这仨儿子、仨儿媳妇是怎么档子事，我全知道。胆儿小的不敢让您进来，怕您死在这儿。您没有病，什么病也没有，素常体格儿也很好，就是饿的！来到我这儿想吃什么给您做什么还不行，饿肚子饿肠子，这一顿多吃一口就撑死！回头您撑死啦，我那仁哥哥来喽准得问我！我先将养您两天再说吧！"

头天，给老太太冲点儿藕粉哪，来点儿茶汤面儿呀；第二天哪，做点儿片儿汤啊，甩个果儿啊；第三天煮点儿挂面哪，包个小饺子儿啊；过了一个礼拜，熬鱼呀；过俩礼拜，燉肉哇；二十多天哪，将养得老太太恢复了原状，精神百倍。这阵儿老太太哪儿也不想去啦，就想在老姑娘这儿住下去啦！

这天她们姑爷有事出去啦，孩子也都睡着啦，夜里头娘儿俩坐在一块儿说闲话儿。老姑娘说："我有一档子事跟您提呀，您可别难过。人生在世界上，养儿得济，养女儿也得济，丈母娘吃姑爷呀，这有的是，不算新鲜；可得分怎么回事，没有儿子成啊，没有儿子能饿死吗？就得吃姑爷。有儿子呀生活困难也可以。您不价，您这仁儿子都有事，都挣钱哪！那还不算，都站着房躺着地，银行里一个人都存一万多呀！您在我这儿这么一住，我们两口子感情好，当然没有说的，夫妻之中啊没有盆儿碗儿不磕不碰的，往后有个抬杠拌嘴哪，您姑爷拿这话一刻薄我，这一句话，我一辈子翻不过身来！我这儿有一个戏法儿，这戏法儿是我变的，您在一边儿给拿着块注单，只要这块注单不打开，打这儿说起呀，儿子，儿媳妇超过二十四孝，大孝格天！孙男弟女呀，在您身边团团乱转，净是顺气的事；可是这注单别打开，一打开，戏法儿漏啦！儿子，儿媳妇拿您不当人，孙男弟女躲着您，没人养活您，在街上要了饭，可别上我这儿来，那怨您把戏法儿变漏啦！"

这阵儿这老太太呀，闺女说什么是什么。怎么个戏法儿呢？如此如彼这么这么档子事。那位说："怎么一档子事呀？"就是回头我说的这档子事。老太太说："行吗？"

"行！"

"好，咱就那么办，闺女！依着你。"

娘儿俩一齐动手。家里有的是劈柴，到厨房先把大灶点上，娘儿俩把屋里所有的锡器家伙——就是出门子时候儿陪送的那四十多斤锡器家伙——完全提到厨房去，把锅烧热了，往里那么一搁就化了。化了之后，姑奶奶就拿火筷子在地下锄了些个坑——长的圆的都有，拿铁杓舀锡汁儿往里倒，凉了拔出来，再往里倒锡汁儿。半宿的工夫全铸得了，长的圆的都有，拿簸箕一撮，撮到炕上。又拿出一丈多白布，给老太太做这么一条斜襟儿褡子，裁好了斜着一缝，有这么宽，把锡饼子、锡条哇弄进一块儿去，把它扒拉到边儿上，四外一纳，再挨着来一块，一块一块，这么一排一排的都缝好。缝得了之后，把老太太上身儿衣裳脱了，把这条褡子往腰里给她这一围，围上之后，系麻花扣子，系上还不成，怕他们解呀！又拿针线都给缝上。往下出溜怎么办？又来两根细带子，十字披红这么一缝，把带子头儿密密地给纳上。把衣掌穿好了，这工夫儿天也就亮啦，给老太太买点儿豆浆买点果子，吃完了，老姑娘拿出十块现洋来，再拿一块钱换成毛票儿、铜子儿，给老太太往兜儿里这么一带，这才给老太太雇车。

您就这么这么办啊，上您大儿子哪儿去，车钱没给，到门口儿您给车钱。"

把老太太搀到车上，老太太上大儿子哪儿去啦！到大儿子门口儿，正赶上大儿媳妇在哪儿买鱼哪，一瞧婆婆来啦，没理。老太太掏钱的时候拿手指头这么一顶啊，嗵！掉地下两块现洋，当啷一见响儿，这拉车的把钱捡起来了："嗵，老太太，您钱掉啦，给您。"

"哎，好好，劳驾劳驾！唉，哪行都有好人，我没瞧见，换别人可就昧起来啦！得啦，谢谢你，啊……三十个子儿雇的，给两毛钱不用找啦！"

两毛！那阵儿一毛钱换五十多铜子儿哪！

儿媳妇一瞧，嗵，这老婆儿开通啊！打腰里一掏钱哗楞哗楞直掉现洋，三十子儿雇的车，两毛钱甭找啦！这……

拉车的才要搀老太太，儿媳妇赶紧过来啦！

"我搀我搀。奶奶您哪儿去啦？我正要接您去哪！我搀您哪！"

搀！搀可是搀，这手抱着孩子，那只手往老太太腰那儿摸去。那位说："儿媳妇儿怎么知道老太太腰里有东西呢？"您听啊！这老太太一边儿走，一边儿拿手直往上掭。那位说："干吗还掭？"四十多斤哪，那玩意儿它沉哪！大奶奶瞧见啦！心说：嗯，腰里有东西，这手抱着孩子，这手一摸呀，硬梆梆地硌手。

"大爷！奶奶来啦！"

这大爷呀打他爸爸死之后没听过这句，光着袜底儿就蹦出来啦！

"啊，妈！您哪儿去啦？我正要接您去哪！哈！"

大奶奶说："你搀着，你搀着！"

"哎！"大爷手往胳肢窝那儿插，大奶奶一撒手，冲大爷一递眼神儿，朝老太太腰那儿努嘴儿，大爷也就明白啦！搀到屋里。

"您坐下，您坐下。"给老太太倒碗茶："您哪儿去啦？正要接您去哪！"

"接我干吗呀，我不是自己个儿来了吗？我的家嘛我不来！孩子，我告诉你呀！世界之上无论男女得有心，没有心可就坏啦！你就拿我说吧，这点儿心哪我算用到啦！你爸爸活着的时候儿呀，我留了点儿心眼儿，这点儿东西哪在你老妹妹那儿搁着，现在我给带来啦！为什么哪？我告诉你，孩子，你可别瞧你给我棒子面儿吃，　吃棒子面儿是没法子，那是你没能耐挣，那没有办法呀！棒子面儿倒管饱哇！我上你二兄弟那儿去，他给我熬粥！事由儿不好也得算着，熬粥，它也是粮食呀！三儿那儿给我铁蚕豆吃，想把我噎死，象话吗！得啦，我谁也不吃累，我把这点儿东西带来呀，谁待我好我找谁。我找你来了！你可听明白了，我可不吃你，你把呀……　哪间房都成，你给我腾出来住，住可是住，我给房钱，该多少钱我给多少钱！雇个老妈子服侍我，做点儿吃的够我们俩吃就成；孩子愿意上我那屋里吃去，我不能往外推，不上我那儿去我可不找。反正这点儿东西呀够我花的，临死哪，剩多剩少，把眼一闭就完啦！给我腾房吧！找老妈儿吧！"

这大儿子在旁边儿一听呀，乒乒乓乓，左右开弓给自个儿来了四个嘴巴：

"妈，妈！您别说啦，您别说啦，您别说啦！多亏这儿没有亲友，要是有亲友听见，人家还拿我当人吗？我还是人吗？您不如给我两刀哪！我不好，招您生气啦，我跪着，您打我一顿出出气，别说这个呀！您住房给钱，这像话吗？这房是您的，连我们的骨头肉儿都是妈妈的！老妈子伺候，老妈子伺候有儿媳妇伺候得好吗？爱吃棒子面儿是您说的，我们哪知道您说反话！您不爱吃棒子面儿您说话呀，这是哪的事？哎，给奶奶炖肉！"

嗬，炖肉啦，立刻就炖肉！炖得啦，老太太这么一吃，吃完了，领老太太到外头听戏去啦，买包厢！听完了戏，在外边儿饭馆吃的晚饭，吃完晚饭回来，太阳还老高哪，这儿把炕铺得了！

"奶奶，您，您睡觉吧，您睡觉吧！"

"干吗这么早睡觉哇？"

"您早早儿睡，养神吧，早点儿睡养神吧！啊，早早儿睡早早儿起呀！"

把老太太搀在炕边儿啦，儿媳妇过来就接拐棍儿，老太太往炕沿上一坐，儿媳妇儿过来就解扣儿，要帮着脱衣裳。

"咦！"老太太站起来啦，一手拿拐棍儿："哎！儿媳妇儿，这可不成啊，你别动我衣裳！我知道，你是好心，你是服侍我，孝顺！衣裳我可不能脱，非脱不成，我可叫警察！一动我衣裳我就走！我告诉你们两人，这点东西是我的命根子，谁动也不成！啊，反正够我后半辈儿花的，死了我就不管啦！动我衣裳，不雇车我也得走！"

大爷说："得啦，您不用着急，妈妈不愿意脱衣裳啊，比脱了衣裳睡更好，省得冻着，得了！"

这一宿哇，这两口子给老太太盖了七回被！那位说："盖被呀？"不是盖，是揭开。灯关了，大爷拿着手电棒儿："奶奶，别踹了被冻着！掖掖，掖掖。"

那儿掖，这儿把被窝掀开，用手电灯照着，摸老太太腰上。摸了半天，研究了半天，把被盖好，溜溜鳅鳅回到屋里，两口子小声儿商量："长的那些个，都是十两的金条，短的那都是五两的；圆的都是锭子，方的是方槽。瞧这意思啊，黄的多，白的少！……别让奶奶生气呀，奶奶要一走，咱们俩可玩儿命，把俩大的叫起来！叫！叫！"

孩子们不醒啊！十五六岁的孩子他跑了一天啦！

"他不醒，明儿一淘气，要把奶奶气跑了这怎么弄？挠脚心，挠脚心！"

一挠脚心，孩子醒啦，孩子才醒，他有个不冲盹儿吗？

"这不是要命吗！又睡啦！"

出去舀碗凉水，含一口，朝着孩子，噗！

"明白过来没有？"

"明白啦！"

"不明白，上院里去转个弯过过风儿再进来！"

"怎么回事呀？"

"怎么回事呀！告诉你们俩儿，你们俩，不算这个小的，打明儿一起，在奶奶跟前的时候，瞧奶奶喜欢，在那儿玩儿，奶奶不喜欢，赶紧走，你奶奶爱听什么说什么，不爱听什么，别说！打明儿起你们谁要招奶奶生了气，奶奶要是一走，不上这儿来啦，你可估摸着，把你们小猴儿崽子撕剥撕剥喂鹰！"

"知道啦，明白啦！"

头天夜里把孩子嘱咐好啦，第二天哪，老太太这两顿饭，点什么给做什么。

才住了四天，也不知道怎么这消息传到二爷耳朵里去啦！二儿子来啦，坐在老太太对过儿哭。老太太说："你跟谁怄气？"

"我跟谁怄气呀？谁跟我怄气呀？我也不去欺负人，人家也不欺负我。外头谈论都骂我，一样都是您的儿子，您老在我哥哥这儿住着，不到我那儿去，那像话吗！您让我在外边儿怎么交朋友！"

把妈妈抢走啦！抢了三天去。大爷又要往回抢，到二爷那儿一看，没啦！一问哪儿去啦？叫三爷那儿抢去啦，又由三爷那儿往回抢。

简断截说吧，这三家儿呀——说一家儿就代表那两家儿啦——全是想吃什么做什么，吃完了听戏呀，看电影儿呀，老早就睡觉，叫老太太脱衣裳，老太太不脱，要叫警察，到哪儿全是这一手儿。你抢过来，他抢过去，哪儿也乱抢，整整齐齐抢了有二年半。有一回这哥儿仨凑到一块儿就合计这个事儿，大爷说："咱们别抢啦，这　么一抢不是让亲友瞧着笑话吗！不就为腰里那点儿东西吗？打这儿起咱们别让她生气，老太太爱什么咱们来什么，尽孝！等到老太太百年之后，咱们三一三剩一就得啦！谁要把老太太气着，老太太说了话啦，说这东西没有谁的，那往后可……可别红眼，老太太只要一有这话，说不给谁谁就完！"

这哥儿俩同意，此后老太太到哪儿哪儿就更孝顺啦。哥儿仨带仨儿媳妇儿，孝顺可是孝顺，就是一个心气儿，什么心气儿哪？盼这老太太早点儿死，一死一分就完啦！

这老太太不但不死啊，倒结实了。老太太怎么到七十多岁倒结实啦？这里头有原因啊，倒结实了。老太太怎么到七十多岁倒结实啦？这里头有原因哪！头一样儿，七十多岁的人顺气，儿子、儿媳妇儿孝顺，孙男弟女全都围着团团乱转，她心里头痛快；第二哪，想吃什么呀，来啦，当时就能吃上，这是结实的第二个原因；第三哪，四十多斤锡饼子老在身上挂着，日久天长那也是锻炼哪！

究竟怎么样哪？"老健春寒秋后暖"，上年纪人过七十啦，处处得讲究卫生，处处得留神。正在二爷这儿住着哪，这天晚上老太太吃东西吃得不消化，又喝了两口温吞水，夜里就跑了三趟厕所。老太太心里明白：上年纪人一宿跑三趟厕所可搁不住哇！回头一躺下，这点儿东西照顾不过来，要是叫儿子、儿媳妇儿给弄下来一瞧是锡饼子，死在街上没人管！这老太太跟她们姑娘定规好了的，老姑娘二年多顶三年没上这儿来，老太太拄着拐棍儿一早儿就出去啦，打腰里掏出一块现洋来，求街坊小孩儿，上哪儿哪儿，门牌多少号，把老姑娘接来。

不到十点钟老姑娘就来啦，到这儿一看，嗬，大爷同着一位西医正进门儿，二爷、三爷也正往外送医生哪，还是两位。怎么回事呀？两位中医呀，二爷、三爷一人请来一位，商量着给开的方子。大爷带着西医进来，看完了也开了方儿，走啦，大夫走了之后，老二就问："老妹妹来啦，咱们按中医这方子抓药哇？还是拿西医这方子抓药？我去吧！"

大爷说："别动，这不是老妹妹在这儿吗，正好！老妹妹不来，还得把老妹妹接来哪，有件事情咱们哥仨合计合计，你们哥儿俩无论如何得帮帮我的忙。咱们四个人哪，脚蹬肩膀儿来的。虽说分了家，不管怎么说也是一父之子，一母所生，你们别让我落骂名啊！我那儿是老宅子，咱们家多少辈儿在那儿住着；我又是长子长门；老太太病到谁家当然都是一样喽，那么要有个百年之后哪，要老在别处住着，我这骂名落得起吗？你们哥儿俩帮我个忙，我赶紧叫辆汽车，把妈妈背上汽车，你们哥儿俩哪，连她们妯娌俩，愿意上我那儿去全去，不愿往我那儿呀！哪天去都成。"

这二爷呀坐在椅子上，理着小胡子，嗬，稳当。"大哥，您这话太光明啦，太磊落啦！可是有一样儿，哈哈，不行！变戏法儿的别瞒打锣的，告诉您实话吧！吃下去顺溜，再吐出来不成！妈妈病在我这儿，那是我运气好，凭天转，转到我这儿啦，打算接走那是不行！"

三爷也抢，老妹妹搭了碴儿："嗨嗨！这要是让街坊听见像话吗？人家不笑话吗？我说，我说。"

"啊，老妹妹说。"

"你们不就是为奶奶腰里这点东西吗？"

"不能！"

"不能什么呀？　我不瞒着，告诉你们实话，老太太腰里那点儿东西原本在我那儿搁着，是跟着我那嫁妆过去的。"

对呀，实话，锡家伙可不是跟着嫁妆过去的吗！

"原本在我那儿搁着，这一回老太太非带走不成，我要不让老太太带，是我贪图是怎么着？我不落那个！让老太太带着上你们这儿来啦！你们哥儿仨谁也别争，谁也别抢，老太太上年纪啦，来回一折腾，老太太受不了！老太太就在二哥这儿养病，二哥呀给找个箱子，把空箱子拿过来咱们都检查检查，看箱子有毛病没有，没有毛病，咱们大家伙看着，把老太太腰里这点东西解下来，搁到箱子里头锁上，锁上可是锁上，钥匙我拿着。你们要是不放心，你们哥儿仨每人再贴道封贴，老太太要是好了哪，咱们再给老太太系到腰里（还留后口哪）；老太太要是有个百年之后哪，这点儿东西呀，听我的吩咐。按规矩说，儿分家女有份，得有我一份儿，可我决不沾一分一厘，娘家东西我不要。那么怎么办哪，这主权可在我这儿，老太太百年之后哇，我瞧你们哥儿仨谁对老的好，谁孝顺，这东西就归谁，要是跟老的一不孝顺，一分一厘也没有他的！"

这哥儿仨一齐伸大拇指："对！对！女英雄！比不了，比不了！咱们就这么办。"

找箱子，把箱子都看完了，老姑娘给老太太脱衣裳，这仨人足这么一忙活，拿小刀儿、剪子，喊哧咔嚓剪开身上的带子，老姑娘把裙子解下来也没让这哥儿仨瞧，呱喳就扔到箱子里啦，盖上盖儿，锁上锁，带起钥匙，这哥儿仨每人贴上条封贴，接碴儿给老太太治病。

怎么样哪？四十来天，医药无效，这老太太死了！嗬！老太太这么一死呀，这大儿子孝顺！大儿子给老太太买的棺材，这棺材是八仙板金丝楠，五寸多厚。铺金盖银，陀罗经被，身底下压七个大金钱，七颗珠子都这么大，要凭他们家底儿，不趁，家里没有现款哪！钱打哪儿来的呢？把房子卖啦，卖房发送妈妈，够孝顺的。这二爷哪，不能再买棺材啦，让大爷占去啦，卖房发送妈妈，够孝顺的。这二爷哪，不能再买棺材啦，让大爷占去啦，能再买口棺材比着吗？搭棚，在二爷家里嘛！起脊大棚，过街牌楼，钟鼓二楼，一殿一卷，门口儿一个大明镜，立个大牌楼，牌楼上写仨大字"当大事"。讲经呢，和尚，老道，喇嘛，尼姑四棚经，搁七七四十九天。二爷的钱也早就花没啦，也是卖房啊！这三的怎么办哪？这三的房早就卖啦，借加一钱，给老太太讲杠，六十四人杠换三班儿，打执事的拉开了走半趟街，金山，银山，烧活。嗬，借印子钱发送妈妈，您就说多孝吧！

不孝能卖房给妈妈买棺材吗？不孝能卖房给妈妈念经吗？不孝能借加一的钱给妈妈讲杠吗？孝顺！孝顺可是孝顺，就一样特别——这么大的白棚啊没人哭！除去烧纸的时候儿老姑奶奶哭两声，余外没人哭。街坊都纳闷，这家儿怎么回事？隔辈人——孙子孙女儿不哭是小孩儿不懂；儿媳妇儿不哭，究竟是抬来的，她跟婆婆不一个心；这儿子横竖是妈养的，他怎么不哭啊？一个眼泪不掉！不但不掉哇，您瞧她那仨儿子，虽说都穿着一身重孝，出来进去谈笑自若；就是胡子碴长点儿。走道腆胸叠肚，嘴里头嘟嘟囔囔，哼哼唧唧唱小曲儿，细这么一听，唱什么哪？《马寡妇开店》。这街坊里头可就有问的，要是问这哥儿仨，妯娌仨，就得问六回，咱问一回就表示全问啦！好比问二爷吧。

"二爷，这棚事办得露脸哪！"

一提露脸，二爷打心里痛快："哈哈，老家儿死了，罪孽深重，提不到露脸！"

"好！听说您不老富裕的，把房子出手啦给妈妈念经，真够孝顺的！"

"那应该应分，房子不算嘛儿，身外之物，再一说是祖产，凭着祖产过日子没有志气，给老的花，正当。"

"孝，孝！我可有句话，这嘴可太直，哈哈，您原谅！"

"什么事？"

"怎么您不哭哇？"

这一说不哭，当时变脸："你这个人，你这个人！说这话像话吗？哭管什么，谁没有个死？我妈妈今年七十四啦，这不是叫老喜丧吗！我们哭？哭也成，我哭死，让我妈活了！不是我们哭死我妈也活不来吗？老喜丧啊，人早晚有个死呀！"

"你怎么乐哪？"

"我怎么不乐呀！不乐像话吗？喜事呀，喜丧嘛我不乐？没有那规矩，有那规矩我们还唱戏哪！您别说这个，您也有老的，他死了也按我们这么办，那就对啦！"

把街坊顶得一愣一愣的。谁一问那就是老喜丧，哥儿仨，妯娌仨一样儿毛病，直到出殡，摔盆儿都没人哭，到坟地下了葬，入土为安哪都没人哭！

埋完了，哥儿仨，妯娌仨就在坟地那儿把孝袍子，孝帽子一脱："老妹妹，老妹妹，上车吧，上车吧，回家吧，回家吧！"

嗬！他们这位老妹妹稳当，坐在坟地那儿："回家？回我们家啦！好几个月，我也够受的啦！"

"甭价，你先回去一趟——先上我们那儿去一趟，去趟啊有点儿事，回头办理完了你再回去歇着，过两天给你道谢！"

"不用，不用，不就是为箱子里那点儿事吗？你们先回去一趟，瞧瞧那封贴扯了没有？"

"我们出来的时候瞧了，封贴没动，封贴没动。"

"封帖没动我就不负责啦！这么着，把钥匙给你们。想当初哇，我有一句话，虽说是儿分产业女有份，我绝对不要那个，我有主权，这东西哪，你们哥儿仨谁对老的最孝顺归谁。到现在一看，你们哥儿仨对老的全孝顺，卖房子发送老的，借加一钱发送老的，都孝顺，我能够向着谁？这么着，你们哥儿仨呀三一三剩一，把它分了，　别给我打份儿，分厘毫丝我不沾。不是封帖没动吗！我没有责任，钥匙交给你们，哥儿仨个分这个别打起来就得！"

"对！对！老妹妹，女中英雄，比不了，比不了！过两天给你道谢！哈！"

这哥儿仨回来啦，进门儿两眼发直，妯娌仨过来就搬箱子，一瞧："封贴没动啊，没人家的责任。"

扯封帖，开开，把那个布褡子抱出来呀往炕上一搁，妯娌仨拿刀子拿剪子喊哧咔嚓剪开了往炕上一倒，唏哩哗啦！这大爷一瞧，站在那儿直嘬牙花子："哎呀，黄的没有，就是白的也能打点儿饥荒，我我我……我说这是银子吗？"

那位三爷机灵："大哥，没错儿没错儿，银子咬不动。"

一听说银子咬不动，哥儿仨，妯娌仨一人拿一块搁嘴里咬，拿出来一瞧，四个牙印儿！

"锡饼子！哎哟，妈呀，这可缺德啦！这是谁出的主意呀？这不是害人吗？妈呀，活不了啦！"

哭上没完啦！

街坊们纳闷呀！街坊们说："这家儿什么毛病啊！妈妈咽气没哭，入殓没哭，摔丧盆儿没哭，怎么完了事哭起来没有完啦！过去劝劝。"

过来一劝。

"哟，要了命啦，您别劝，活不了啦，妈妈死了死了吧，这怎么活呀？"

"不是老喜丧吗？"

"老喜丧，这帐没法儿还哪！"

Appendix 3

Chinese text for "Listening to the Bells at Sword Pavilion"

剑阁闻铃

清　韩小窗

I.

1. 马嵬坡下草青青，
   今日犹存妃子陵。

2. 题壁有诗皆抱恨，
   入祠无客不伤情。

3. 万里西巡君请去，
   何劳雨夜叹闻铃。

4. 杨贵妃梨花树下香魂散，
   陈元礼带领着军卒保驾行。

II.

5. 叹君王，万种凄凉，千般寂寞，
   一心似醉，两泪如倾。

6. 愁漠漠，残月晓星初领略，
   路迢迢，涉水登山哪惯经。

7. 好容易，盼到了行宫，歇歇倦体，
   偏遇着，冷雨凄风助惨情。

8. 剑阁中，有怀不寐唐天子，
   听窗外，不住地叮当连连地作响声。

9. 忙问道："外面的声音却是何物也？"
   高力士奏："林中的雨点和檐下的金铃。"

10. 这君王，一闻此言（哪）长吁短叹（哪）
    说："正是，断肠人听断肠声（啊）！"

III.

11. 似这般， 不作美的铃声，不作美的雨（啊，
    怎当我，割不断的相思，割不断的情。

12. 洒窗棂， 点点 敲人心欲碎，
    摇落木，声声使我梦难成。

13. 噹嘟嘟，惊魂响自檐前起，
    冰凉凉，彻骨寒从被底生。

14. 孤灯儿照我人单影，
    雨夜同谁话五更。

15. 从古来，巫山曾入襄王梦，
    我何以，欲梦卿时梦不成。

16. 莫不是，弓鞋懒踏三更月，
    莫不是，衫袖难禁午夜风。

17. 莫不是，旅馆萧条卿嫌闷，
    莫不是，兵马奔驰心怕惊。

18. 莫不是，芳卿心内怀余恨，
    莫不是，薄幸心中少至诚。

19. 既不然，神女因何不离洛浦，
    空教我，流干了眼泪望断了魂灵。

IV.

20. 一个儿，枕冷衾寒卧红罗帐里，
    一个儿，珠沉玉碎埋黄土堆中。

21. 连理枝，暴雨摧残分左右，
    比翼鸟，狂风吹散各西东。

22. 料今生璧合无期，珠还无日，
    但只愿，泉下追随伴玉容。

23. 料芳卿，自是嫦娥归月殿，
    早知道，半途而废又何必西行。

24. 悔不该，兵权错付卿义子，
    悔不该，国事全凭你从兄。

25. 细思量，都是奸贼他把国误，
    真冤枉，偏说妃子你倾城。

26. 众三军，何仇何恨和卿作对，
    可愧我，想保你的残生也是不能。

27. 可怜你，香魂一缕随风散，
    却使我，血泪千行似雨倾。

28. 恸临危，直瞪瞪的星眸，咯吱吱的皓齿，
    战兢兢的玉体，惨淡淡的花容。

29. 眼睁睁，既不能救你又不能替你，
    悲恸恸，将何以酬卿又何以对卿。

30. 最伤心，一年一度梨花放，
    从今后，一见梨花一惨情。

31. 我的妃子（啊），一时顾命诬害了你，
    好教我，追悔新情（啊）忆旧情。

V.

32. 再不能，太液池观莲并蒂，
    再不能，沉香亭谱调清平。

33. 再不能，玩月楼头同玩月，
    再不能，长生殿内祝长生。

34. 我二人，夜深私语到情浓处，
    你还说，恩爱的夫妻世世同。

35. 到如今，言犹在耳人何处，
    几度思量几恸情。

36. 窗儿外，铃声儿断续那雨声更紧，
    房儿内，残灯儿半灭御榻如冰。

37. 柔肠儿，九转百结百结欲断，
    泪珠儿，千行万点万点通红。

38. 这君王，一夜无眠悲哀到晓，
    猛听得，内宦启奏，请驾登程。

Appendix 4

Comparison of vocal lines for Luo and Liu schools ("At Break of Day")

T-3 Lu:

jià - shà - ang dē jīn jī - - - bú zhù dē lián shē - eng chàng.

T-3 Xiao:

jià shà - ang de jīn jī bú zhù de lián___ shē - eng___ chàng.___

B-3 Lu:

qiān___ mén kaī___ wàn___ hù___ fāng, zhè cai jīng dò-ng liaǒ - xíng lù___

zhǐ fen___ jī___ jī máng máng dǎ diǎn zhē xíng náng chū lǐ liaǒ dǐ du fáng goù bēn li-

aǒ qián biān nà___ f___ zuǒ cūn___ (mei) - - - zhuāng___

B-3 Xiao:

qiān mén kaī wàn hù fāng, zhè___ jīng___ dòng liaò___ nà xíng lù de

zhí-zǐ jī___ ji máng máng huǎng__fi huǎng dāng dǎ diǎn liaò xíng náng___ chū lǐ liaò

diàn___ fáng goù bēn___ liaò___ qián___ biān nà yī___ zuǒ - cū-un (mei) - zhuāng

xiù___ fáng___ de‑jiā rér yaǒ, zaǒ ‑ ‑ ‑ qǐ_____

xiù fáng de___ jiā ré ‑ er___ yaǒ,___ zaǒ ‑ qǐ_____

wǒ zhǐ ‑ jiàn tā miàn duì líng huā___ yú ‑ un fēn

liǎng___ bìn de bìn shàng daǐ zhě xiān huā, huā___ zhǐ zhaǒ zhǎn ne, tā shǐ

qiaǒ ‑ ‑ ‑ shū ‑ ‑ ‑ zhuāng.

wǒ zhǐ ‑ jiàn___ tā miàn___ duì zhě líng huā___ yú ‑ un fēn

liǎng___ bìn de bìn shàng daǐ zhě xiān___ huā, huā___ zhǐ zhaǒ zhǎn ne zhě shǐ

qiaǒ ‑ ‑ ‑ shū ‑ ‑ ‑ zhuāng

Appendix 5

Musical transcription of "Listening to the Bells at Sword Pavilion"

chéng   Jǐ bù rán   shēn nǚ   yīn hé   bù lí luò

pǔ   Kōng jiào wǒ   liú   gān liao yǎn leì

wàng duàn le hún   líng

Yí gè

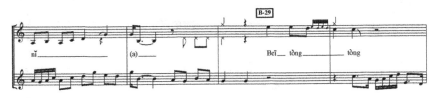

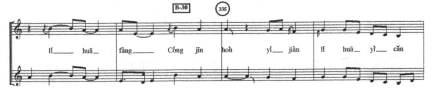

Zhè   jūn   wǎng___   yí___   yè___   wú   mián___   bēi   aī___   daò___

xiaǒ_____   Mèng___   tīng___   dé___   neǐ___   huàn___   qǐ___   zoù___

qǐng___   jià___   dēng   chéng_____

Appendix 6

Glossary of selected Chinese characters

Bai Niu shuoshu	白妞说书
Changbanpo	长板坡
Choumo yinchu	丑末寅初
Dan	旦
Dankou xiangsheng	单口相声
Danxiar	单弦儿
Dougende	逗哏的
Dushiniang	杜十娘
Duikou xiangsheng	对口相声
Hualaqiar	化蜡扦儿
Jiange wenling	剑阁闻铃
Jingyundagu	京韵大鼓
Laocan youji	老残游记
Liu Baoquan	刘宝全
Liu E (Tieyun)	刘鹗（鐵雲）
Liu Xiumei	刘秀梅
Lu Xun	鲁迅
Lu Yiqin	陆倚琴
Luo Yusheng	骆玉笙
Mei Lanfang	梅兰芳
Penggende	捧哏的
Qi	气
Qingbai	清白
Qingyi	青衣
Quyi	曲艺
Ruan Lingyu	阮玲玉
Shi Huiru	石慧儒
Tianjin shidiao	天津时调
Wang Yubao	王毓宝
Xianshi	弦师
Xiangsheng	相声
Xue Baokun	薛宝琨
Yitouchen	一头沉

Yueju	越	剧	
Zhang Cuifeng	章	翠	风
Zhu Xueying	朱	学	颖
Zidishu	子	弟	书
Zimugen	子	母	哏

References

Chinese language sources

An, Baoyong. 2009. "Wo xiaide Wang Yubao yu Tianjin shidiao" (My Beloved Wang Yubao and Tianjin Popular Tunes). *Zhongguo quyijia xiehui* (Chinese *Quyi* Workers' Association) 4 :18–19.

Chen, Chen. 2013. "Tianjin shidiao yinyuefazhan kao" (An Investigation into the Musical Development of Tianjin Popular Tunes). M.A. Thesis, Tianjin yinyuexueyuan (Tianjin Conservatory of Music).

Cui, Yunhua. 2005. *Shuzhai yu shufang zhi jian: Qingday zidishu yanjiu* (Between the Study and the Library: Research on Qing dynasty Manchu Ballads). Beijing: Zhongguo zhengfa daxue chubanshe (Chinese University of Political Science and Law Press).

Gang, Zi. 2008. "Wang Yubao yu Tianjin shidiao yantaohui zai Jin juxing" (A Discussion in Tianjin about Wang Yubao and Tianjin Popular Tunes). *Zhongguo quyijia xiehui* 11: 79.

Gong, Xin. 1999. *Luo Yusheng yanchang Jingyundagu xuanji* (Selected Works from Luo Yusheng's Beijing Drumsong Repertoire). Beijing: Dazhong wenyi (Popular Literature and Arts Press).

Hua, Xiaobao. 1991. Interview with the author. Tianjin, China (January 4).

Jia, Liqing. 2008. *Luo Yusheng nianpu* (A Chronicle of the Life of Luo Yusheng). Tianjin: Tianjin Renmin (Tianjin People's Press).

Liu, Shufang. 1983. "Luo Yusheng changqiang yanjiu" (A Study of Luo Yusheng's Melodic Style). *Yinyue yanjiu* (Music Research Institute) 3: 92–104.

Liu, Xiumei. 1985. Interview with author. Nankai University, Tianjin, China (December 23).

Lu, Xun. 1981 "Lun zhaoxiang zhi lei" (Discussing Photography and Such). Originally written in 1924. In *Lu Xun Quan Ji* (Collected Works of Lu Xun). 1981. Beijing: Renmin wenxue chubanshe: 287–294.

Lu, Yiqin. 1991. Interview with author. Tianjin, China (January 4).

Luo, Junsheng. 2009. "Gen Shi Huirulaoshi xuechang Danxian" (Studying Danxian with Teacher Shi Huiru). *Zhongguo quyijia xiehui* 10: 28–29.

Luo, Yusheng, as told to Meng Ran. 1993. *Tanban xiange qishiqiu* (70 Years as a Drumsong Performer). Beijing: Xinhua (New China Press).

———. 2003. *Luo Yusheng Jingyundagu zhenban diancang* (Collector's Edition of Luo Yusheng's Greatest Beijing Drumsong Performances), vols. 1–4. Beijing: China Record Company. CD.

Meng, Ran and Luo Junsheng, eds. 2012. *Luo Yusheng chuanqi* (Remembrances of Luo Yusheng). Tianjin: Tianjin Renmin.

Nan, Hongyan and Qian Guozhen. 1999. "Zhuming Jingyundagu biaoyan yishushenghuo nianbiao" (A Chronology of the Artistic Career of the Celebrated Performing Artist Luo Yusheng). *Yinyue xueyuan xuebao (Tianjin)* (Journal of the Tianjin Music Research Institute).

Sun, Fuhai. 2008. "Qubujingren shibuxiu—Ji Zhongguoquyi mudanjiang zhongshenchengjiujiang huodezhe Wang Yubao" (We Can't Rest Until the Music has Moved Everyone: Remembering Wang Yubao, Winner of the Chinese *Quyi* Peony Award for Lifetime Achievement). *Zhongguo quyijia xiehui* 10: 38–42.

Tao, Dun. 1983. *Luo Yusheng yanchang Jingyundagu xuan* (A Selection of Luo Yusheng's Beijing Drumsong Pieces). Tianjin: Baihua (Hundred Flowers Press).

Wang, Yubao. 1991. Interview with author. Tianjin, China (January 2).

Wu, Wenke. 2012. "Cong Jingyundagu 'Luo (Yusheng) pai' de xingcheng kan Quyi ruhe jichenghe chuangxin: xie zai Jingyundagu yanchang yishujia Luo Yusheng shishi" (How Can *Quyi* Carry On and Blaze New Trails in the Development of Luo Yusheng's School of Beijing Drum Song: Written on the Tenth Anniversary of Luo Yusheng's Passing). *Quyi luntan (Quyi* Discussions) 10: 20–23.

Xiao, Xia. 2007. "Wo he Shi Huiru laoshide yilu" (Teacher Shi Huiru's Artistic Road and I). *Zhongguo quyijia xiehui* 3: 48–49.

Xue, Baokun. 1984. *Luo Yusheng he tade Jingyundagu* (Luo Yusheng and her Beijing Drum Song). Harbin, China: Heilongjiang Renmin (Heilongjiang People's Press).

Xue, Baokun. 1985a Interview with author. Tianjin, China (October 6).

———. 1985b Interview with author. Tianjin, China (November 1).

———. 1985c Interview with author. Tianjin, China (November 9).

———. 1985d Interview with author. Tianjin, China (November 23).

———. 1985e Interview with author. Tianjin, China (December 18).

———. 1985f Interview with author. Tianjin, China (December 23).

———. 1986a Interview with author. Tianjin, China (March 5).

———. 1986b Interview with author. Tianjin, China (April 16).

———. 1986c Interview with author. Tianjin, China (July 7).

———. 1991 Interview with author. Tianjin, China (January 3).

Yao, Xiyun. 1981. "Tianjin shidiaode yanbian" (Changes in the Performance of Tianjin Shidiao). In *Tianjin wenshi ziliao xuanji* 14: 160–169.

Zhang, Geng, ed. 1983. *Zhongguo Dabaike Quanshu: Xiju Quyi* (The Encyclopedia Sinica: Operatic and Narrative Arts Volume). Beijing: Zhongguo dabaike quanshu chubanshe.

Zhao, Lixin, director. 2012. *Fenmochunqiuzhi Jingyun mingjia Xiao Caiwu-Luo Yusheng* (Master Performer Xiao Caiwu-Luo Yusheng as She Ascends the Stage in Her Advanced Years). Documentary. Beijing: Beijing Television.

Zhongguo Quyixie Liaoningfenhui (Liaoning Branch of the Chinese *Quyi* Arts Workers Association). 1979. *Zidishu xuan* (Collection of Manchu Ballads). Liaoning: Zhongguo quyigongzuozhe xiehui fenhui (The Liaoning Branch of the Chinese *Quyi* Worker's Association Press).

Zhou, Licheng. 2010. "Wang Yubao yu Tianjin shidiao" (Wang Yubao and Tianjin Popular Tunes). *Zhongguo dangan baoshe* (Office of Chinese Newspaper Archives) 19: 3 (August).

Zhu, Xueying. 1985. *Bai Niu shuoshu* (Bai Niu Tells a Story). Beijing: Zhongguo Quyi chubanshe (Chinese *Quyi* Press).

English language sources

Abbate, Carolyn. 1995. "Opera, Or the Envoicing of Women." In *Musicology and Difference: Gender and Sexuality in Music Scholarship*, edited by Ruth A. Solie, 225–258. Berkeley: University of California Press.

———. 1996. *Unsung Voices: Opera and Musical Narrative in the Nineteenth Century.* Princeton: Princeton University Press.

Abu-Lughod, Lila. 1999. *Veiled Sentiments: Honor and Poetry in a Bedouin Society.* Los Angeles: University of California Press.

Ancelet, Barry Jean. 2007. "Falling Apart to Stay Together: Deep Play in the Grand Marais Mardi Gras." In *The Performance Studies Reader*, 2nd ed., edited by Henry Bial, 164–173. New York: Routledge.

Armstrong, Paul B. 2013. *How Literature Plays with the Brain: The Neuroscience of Reading and Art.* Baltimore: Johns Hopkins University Press.

Austern, Linda Phyllis. 1989. "'Sing Again Syren': The Female Musician and Sexual Enchantment in Elizabethan Life and Literature." *Renaissance Quarterly* 42 (3): 420–448.

———. 1996. "'No Women Are Indeed': The Boy Actor as Vocal Seductress in Late Sixteenth-and Early Seventeenth-Century English Drama." In *Embodied Voices: Representing Female Vocality in Western Culture*, edited by Leslie C. Dunn and Nancy A. Jones, 83–102. Cambridge: Cambridge University Press.

Austern, Linda Phyllis and Inna Naroditskaya. 2006. "Introduction." In *Music of the Sirens*, edited by Linda Phyllis Austern and Inna Naroditskaya, 1–15. Bloomington: Indiana University Press.

Bao, Juemin and He Ziqiang. 1983. "The Characteristics and Prospects of the City Development of Tianjin." Paper presented at the UNU-CAS Workshop on Regional Development Planning. Beijing, 29 March.

Barlow, Tani E. 1994. "Theorizing Woman: *Funü, Guojia, Jiating.*" In *Body, Subject & Power in China*, edited by Angela Zito and Tani E. Barlow, 253–290. Chicago: University of Chicago Press.

Barthes, Roland. 1977. *Image, Music, Text.* Translated by Stephen Heath. New York: Hill and Wang.

Bartoli, Cecilia. 2009. *Sacrificium: The Art of the Castrati.* Directed by Olivier Simonnet. London: Decca DVD.

Baudrillard, Jean. 2010. *Simulacra and Simulation.* Translated by Sheila Faria Glaser. Ann Arbor: University of Michigan Press.

Bergeron, Katherine. 1996. "The Castrato as History." *Cambridge Opera Journal* 8 (2): 167–184.

Blacking, John. 1995. *Music, Culture, and Experience: Selected Papers of John Blacking.* Chicago: University of Chicago Press.

Bordahl, Vibeke and Margaret B. Wan. 2010. *The Interplay of the Oral and the Written in Chinese Popular Literature* (Nias Studies in Asian Topics). Honolulu: University of Hawaii Press.

Bossler, Beverly. 2013. *Courtesans, Concubines, and the Cult of Female Fidelity.* Cambridge: Harvard University Press.

Brindley, Erica Fox. 2012. *Music, Cosmology, and the Politics of Harmony in Early China.* Albany: State University of New York Press.

Brownell, Susan and Jeffrey N. Wasserstrom. 2002. *Chinese Masculinities/Chinese Femininities: A Reader.* Berkeley: University of California Press.

Bruner, Edward M. 1986. "Experience and Its Expression." In *The Anthropology of Experience*, edited by Victor W. Turner and Edward M. Bruner, 1–30. Urbana: University of Illinois Press.

Butler, Judith. 1988. "Performative Acts and Gender Constitution: An Essay in Phenomenology and Feminist Criticism." *Theatre Journal* 40: 519–531.

———. 1997. *Excitable Speech: A Politics of the Performative.* New York: Routledge.

———. 2007. "Performative Acts and Gender Constitution: An Essay in Phenomenology and Feminist Theory." In *The Performance Studies Reader*, edited by Henry Bial, 2nd edition, 187–199. New York: Routledge.

Cahill, Ann J. and Jennifer Hansen. 2003. "Introduction." In *Continental Feminism Reader*, edited by Ann J. Cahill and Jennifer Hansen, 1–21. Lanham, MD: Rowman and Littlefield Publishers.

Chow, Rey. 1991. *Woman and Chinese Modernity: The Politics of Reading Between East and West.* Minneapolis: University of Minnesota Press.

———. 1997. *Primitive Passions.* New York: Columbia University Press.

Clément, Catherine. 1988. *Opera, or the Undoing of Women.* Translated by Betsy Wing. Minneapolis: University of Minnesota Press.

Cornell, Drucilla. 1991. *Beyond Accommodation. Ethical Feminism, Deconstruction and the Law.* New York: Routledge.

Creed, Barbara. 2007. *The Monstrous-Feminine: Film, Feminism, Psychoanalysis.* New York: Routledge.

Cross, Ian. 2012. "Music as a Social and Cognitive Process." In *Language and Music as Cognitive Systems*, edited by Patrick Rebuschat, Martin Rohrmeier, John Hawkins, and Ian Cross, 315–328. Oxford: Oxford University Press.

Cross, Ian and Iain Morley. 2010. "The Evolution of Music: Theories, Definitions and the Nature of the Evidence." In *Communicative Musicality: Exploring the Basis of Human Companionship*, edited by Stephen Malloch and Colwyn Trevarthen, 61–82. Oxford: Oxford University Press.

Danielson, Virginia. 1997. *The Voice of Egypt: Umm Kulthūm, Arabic Song, and Egyptian Society in the Twentieth Century.* Chicago: University of Chicago Press.

Dayan, Peter. 2006. *Music Writing Literature: From Sand via Debussy to Derrida.* Aldershot, UK: Ashgate.

De Bary, William T. 2001. *Sources of Chinese Tradition: From 1600 Through the Twentieth Century,* Volume 2, 2nd ed. New York: Columbia University Press.

DeWoskin, Kenneth J. 1982. *A Song for One or Two: Music and the Concept of Art in Early China.* Ann Arbor: Center for Chinese Studies, University of Michigan.

Dissanayake, Ellen. 2000. "Antecedents of the Temporal Arts in Early Mother-Infant Interaction." In *The Origins of Music*, edited by Nils L. Wallin, Bjorn Merker, and Steven Brown, 389–410. Cambridge, MA: The MIT Press.

———. 2010. "Root, Leaf, Blossom, or Bole: Concerning the Origin and Adaptive Function of Music." In *Communicative Musicality: Exploring the Basis of Human Companionship*, edited by Stephen Malloch and Colwyn Trevarthen, 17–30. Oxford: Oxford University Press.

Dudden, Faye. 1994. *Women in the American Theater: Actresses and Audiences, 1790–1870.* New Haven: Yale University Press.

Dunn, Leslie C. and Nancy A. Jones, eds. 2001. *Embodied Voices: Representing Female Vocality in Western Culture.* Cambridge: Cambridge University Press.

Engh, Barbara 2001. "Adorno and the Sirens: Tele-Phono-Graphic Bodies." In *Embodied Voices: Representing Female Vocality in Western Culture*, edited by

Leslie C. Dunn and Nancy A. Jones, 120–135. Cambridge: Cambridge University Press.

Freitas, Roger. 2009. *Portrait of a Castrato: Politics, Patronage, and Music in the Life of Atto Melani (1626–1714)*. Cambridge: Cambridge University Press.

Fujita, Minoru. 2006. "Onnagata in Kabuki and the London Globe Theatre." In *Transvestism and the Onnagata Traditions in Shakespeare and Kabuki*, edited by Minoru Fujita and Michael Shapiro, 132–158. Kent, UK: Global Oriental.

Furth, Charlotte. 1999. *A Flourishing Yin: Gender in China's Medical History, 960–1665*. Berkeley: University of California Press.

Gallagher, Lowell. 1995. "Jenny Lind and the Voice of America." In *En Travesti: Women, Gender Subversion, Opera*, edited by Corinne E. Blackmer and Patricia Juliana Smith, 190–215. New York: Columbia University Press.

Gold, Thomas, Doug Guthrie, and David Wank, eds. 2008. *Social Connections in China: Institutions, Culture, and the Changing Nature of Guanxi*. New York: Cambridge University Press.

Goldman, Andrea S. 2012. *Opera and the City: The Politics of Culture in Beijing, 1770–1900*. Stanford: Stanford University Press.

Goldstein, Joshua. 2007. *Drama Kings: Players and Publics in the Re-creation of Peking Opera, 1870–1937*. Berkeley: University of California Press.

Gould, Jonathan. 2007. *Can't Buy Me Love: The Beatles, Britain, and America*. New York: Harmony Books.

Harris, Rachel and Rowan Pease. 2013. "Introduction." In *Gender in Chinese Music*, edited by Rachel Harris, Rowan Pease, and Shzr Ee Tan, 1–25. Rochester: University of Rochester Press.

Heller, Wendy. 2003. *Emblems of Eloquence: Opera and Women's Voices in Seventeenth-Century Venice*. Berkeley: University of California Press.

Herbert, Emily. 2010. *Lady Gaga: Queen of Pop*. London: John Blake Publishing.

Herbert, Ruth. 2011. *Everyday Music Listening: Absorption, Dissociation and Trancing*. Farnham, UK: Ashgate.

Hershatter, Gail. 1986. *The Workers of Tianjin, 1900–1949*. Stanford: Stanford University Press.

———. 2007. *Women in China's Long Twentieth Century*. Los Angeles: University of California Press.

Holford-Strevens, Leofranc. 2006. "Sirens in Antiquity and the Middle Ages." In *Music of the Sirens*, edited by Linda Phyllis Austern and Inna Naroditskaya, 16–51. Bloomington: Indiana University Press.

Hung, William. 1952. *Tu Fu: China's Greatest Poet*. Cambridge: Harvard University Press.

Hutcheon, Linda. 2013. *A Theory of Adaptation*, 2nd ed. New York: Routledge.

Jiang, Jin. 2009. *Women Playing Men: Yue Opera and Social Change in Twentieth-Century Shanghai*. Seattle: University of Washington Press.

Kano, Ayako. 2001. *Acting Like a Woman in Modern Japan: Theater, Gender, and Nationalism*. New York: Palgrave.

Ko, Dorothy and Wang Zheng. 2007. "Introduction: Translating Feminisms in China." In *Translating Feminisms in China*, edited by Dorothy Ko and Wang Zheng, 1–12. Malden, MA: Blackwell Publishing Ltd.

Kominz, Laurence R. 1997. *The Stars Who Created Kabuki: Their Lives, Loves and Legacy*. Tokyo: Kodansha International.

Koskoff, Ellen. 2014. *A Feminist Ethnomusicology: Writings on Music and Gender.* Urbana: University of Illinois Press.

Koestenbaum, Wayne. 2001. *The Queen's Throat: Opera, Homosexuality, and The Mystery of Desire.* New York: Da Capo Press.

Kristeva, Julia. 1980. *Desire in Language: A Semiotic Approach to Literature and Art.* Translated by Thomas Gora, Alice Jardine, and Leon Roudiez, edited by Leon Roudiez. New York: Columbia University Press.

———. 1982. *Powers of Horror: An Essay on Abjection.* Translated by Leon S. Roudiez. New York: Columbia University Press.

———. 1984. *Revolution in Poetic Language.* Translated by Margaret Waller with an Introduction by Leon S. Roudiez. New York: Columbia University Press.

———. 1987. *Tales of Love.* Translated by Leon S. Roudiez. New York: Columbia University Press.

———. 1989. *Black Sun: Depression and Melancholia.* Translated by Leon S. Roudiez. New York: Columbia University Press.

Lawson, Francesca R. Sborgi. 2011. *The Narrative Arts of Tianjin: Between Music and Language.* Farnham, UK: Ashgate.

———. 2012. "Consilience Revisited: Musical and Scientific Approaches to Chinese Performance." *Ethnomusicology* 56 (1): 86–111.

———. 2014a. "Bai Niu and the Women of *Quyi*: Appropriating Metaphysical Femininity and Reclaiming the Feminine Voice in Republican China." *Modern Chinese Literature and Culture* 26 (1): 41–70.

———. 2014b. "Is Music an Adaptation or a Technology? Ethnomusicological Perspectives from the Analysis of Chinese *Shuochang*." *Ethnomusicology Forum* 23 (1): 3–26.

Li, Siu Leung. 2006. *Cross Dressing in Chinese Opera.* Hong Kong: Chinese University Press.

Li, Wai-Yee. 1997. "The Late Ming Courtesan: Invention of a Cultural Ideal." In *Writing Women in Late Imperial China*, edited by Ellen Widmer and Kang-I Sun Chang, 46–73. Stanford: Stanford University Press.

Link, Perry. 1980. "Hou Baolin: An Appreciation." *Chinese Literature* 2: 84–94.

———. 1984. "The Genie and the Lamp: Revolutionary *Xiangsheng*." In *Popular Chinese Literature and Performing Arts in the People's Republic of China, 1949–1979*, edited by Bonnie McDougall, 83–111. Los Angeles: University of California Press.

———. 1986. "Stuck in Xiangsheng." *Chinoperl Papers* 14: 27–36.

Liu, E. [1907] 1990. *The Travels of Lao Tsan* (Lao Can). Translated by Harold Shadick. New York: Columbia University Press.

Liu, James J.Y. 1974. *The Art of Chinese Poetry.* Chicago: University of Chicago Press.

Lu, Yu. 1973 *The Old Man Who Does as He Pleases: Selections from the Poetry and Prose of Lu Yu.* Translated by Burton Watson. New York: Columbia University Press.

Ma, Haili. 2015. *Urban Politics and Cultural Capital: The Case of Chinese Opera.* Farnham: Ashgate.

Malloch, Stephen and Colwyn Trevarthen. 2010. "Musicality: Communicating the Vitality and Interests of Life." In *Communicative Musicality: Exploring the Basis of Human Companionship*, 1–11. Oxford: Oxford University Press.

Mann, Susan. 2011. *Gender and Sexuality in Modern Chinese History.* Cambridge: Cambridge University Press.

Mann, Susan and Yu-Yin Cheng. 2001. "Editor's Introduction." In *Under Confucian Eyes: Writings on Gender in Chinese History*, edited by Susan Mann and Yu-Yin Cheng, 1–8, Berkeley: University of California Press.

McClary, Susan. 1988. "Foreword, The Undoing of Opera: Toward a Feminist Criticism of Music." In Catherine Clément, *Opera, or the Undoing of Women*. Translated by Betsy Wing, ix-xviii. Minneapolis: University of Minnesota Press.

McKenzie, Jon. 2001. *Perform or Else: From Discipline to Performance*. New York: Routledge.

McMahon, Keith. 1994. "The Classic 'Beauty-Scholar' Romance and the Superiority of the Talented Woman." In *Body, Subject and Power in China*, edited by Angela Zito and Tani E. Barlow, 227–52. Chicago: University of Chicago Press.

Miller, Geoffrey. 2000. "Evolution of Human Music through Sexual Selection" In *The Origins of Music*, edited by Nils L. Wallin, Björn Merker, and Steven Brown, 329–360. Cambridge, MA: The MIT Press.

Mithen, Steven. 2006. *The Singing Neanderthals: The Origins of Music, Language, Mind, and Body*. Cambridge: Harvard University Press.

Mordden, Ethan. 1990. *Demented: A Provocative Inside Look at Opera's Greatest Divas—from Nellie Melba to Maria Callas, from Adelina Patti to Joan Sutherland*. New York: Simon and Schuster.

Morley, Iain. 2013. *The Prehistory of Music: Human Evolution, Archaeology, and the Origins of Musicality*. Oxford: Oxford University Press.

Moser, David. 1990. "Reflexivity in the Humor of *Xiangsheng*." *Chinoperl Papers* 15: 45–68.

Murphy, Robert F. 1957. "Intergroup Hostility and Social Cohesion," *American Anthropologist* 59: 1018–1035.

———. 1973. "Social Structure and Sex Antagonism." In *Peoples and Cultures of Native South America*, edited by Daniel A. Gross, 213–224. Garden City, NY: Doubleday and the Natural History Press.

Nettl, Bruno. 1985. *The Western Impact on World Music*. New York: Schirmer Books.

Nye, Andrea. 1987. "Woman Clothed with the Sun: Julia Kristeva and the Escape from/to Language." *Signs* 12 (4): 664–686.

Oliver, Kelly. 1993. *Reading Kristeva: Unraveling the Double Bind*. Bloomington: Indiana University Press.

Olivova, Lucie. 2004. "Chinese and Japanese Storytelling: Selected Topical Bibliography of the Works of Vena Hrdlickova and Zdenek Hrdlicka." *Chinoperl Papers* 25: 87–97.

Orgel, Stephen. 1996. *Impersonations*. Cambridge: Cambridge University Press.

Patel, Aniruddh D. 2008. *Music, Language, and the Brain*. Oxford: Oxford University Press.

Pian, Rulan Chao. 1979. "Musical Analysis of the Medley Song, *The Courtesan's Jewel Box*." *Chinoperl Papers* 9: 9–31.

———. 2011. "Northern Prosimetric: A Medley Song from Northern China." In *The Columbia Anthology of Chinese Folk and Popular Literature*, edited by Victor H. Mair and Mark Bender, 314–325. New York: Columbia University Press.

Pinker, Steven. 2009. *How the Mind Works*. New York: W.W. Norton.

Poizat, Michel. 1992. *The Angel's Cry: Beyond the Pleasure Principle in Opera*. Translated by Arthur Denner. Ithaca: Cornell University Press.

Prest, Julia. 2006. *Theatre under Louis XIV: Cross-Casting and the Performance of Gender in Drama, Ballet and Opera*. New York: Palgrave Macmillan.

Rebollo-Sborgi, Francesca (Francesca R. Sborgi Lawson). 2001. "The Manchu Legacy in Chinese Oral Narrative." In *Altaic Affinities: Proceedings of the 40th Meeting of the Permanent International Altaistic Conference (PIAC)*, edited by David B. Honey and David C. Wright, 258–66. Bloomington: Indiana University Research Institute for Inner Asian Studies.

Robertson, Carol E. 1989. "Power and Gender in the Musical Experiences of Women." In *Women and Music in Cross-Cultural Perspective*, edited by Ellen Koskoff, 225–244. Urbana: University of Illinois Press.

Robertson, Jennifer. 1998. *Sexual Politics and Popular Culture in Modern Japan.* Berkeley: University of California Press.

Robinson, Paul. 1988. "A Deconstructive Postscript: Reading Libretti and Misreading Opera." In *Reading Opera*, edited by Arthur Groos and Roger Parker, 328–346. Princeton: Princeton University Press.

Ropp, Paul S. 1997. "Ambiguous Images of Courtesan Culture in Late Imperial China." In *Writing Women in Late Imperial China*, edited by Ellen Widmer and Kang-I Sun Chang, 17–45. Stanford: Stanford University Press.

Rutherford, Susan. 2006. *The Prima Donna and Opera, 1815–1930.* Cambridge: Cambridge University Press.

Schalow, Paul G. 2006. "Figures of Worship: Responses to Onnagata on the Kabuki Stage in Seventeenth-century Japanese Vernacular Prose." In *Transvestism and the Onnagata Traditions in Shakespeare and Kabuki*, edited by Minoru Fujita and Michael Shapiro, 59–69. Kent, UK: Global Oriental.

Schechner, Richard. 1998. "What Is Performance Studies Anyway?" In *The Ends of Performance*, edited by Peggy Phelan and Jill Lane, 357–362. New York: New York University Press.

Schippers, Birgit. 2011. *Julia Kristeva and Feminist Thought.* Edinburgh: Edinburgh University Press.

Scott, Mary. 1991. "Portraits of Women in Zidishu," Unpublished manuscript, April 1991.

Shapiro, Michael. 2006. "The Introduction of Actresses in England: Delay or Defensiveness?" In *Transvestism and the Onnagata Traditions in Shakespeare and Kabuki*, edited by Fujita Minoru and Michael Shapiro, 33–58. Kent, UK: Global Oriental.

Silverman, Kaja. 1988. *The Acoustic Mirror: The Female Voice in Psychoanalysis and Cinema.* Bloomington: Indiana University Press.

Smart, Mary Ann. 1995. "The Lost Voice of Rosine Stoltz." In *En Travesti: Women, Gender Subversion, Opera*, edited by Corinne E. Blackmer and Patricia Julianna Smith, 169–181. New York: Columbia University Press.

Sommer, Matthew H. 2000. *Sex, Law, and Society in Late Imperial China.* Stanford: Stanford University Press.

Stark, Steven D. 2005. *Meet the Beatles: A Cultural History of the Band that Shook Youth, Gender, and the World.* New York: Harper Entertainment.

Stevens, Catherine. 1975. *Peking Drumsinging*, Ph.D. dissertation, Harvard University.

———. 1990. "The Slopes of Changban: A Beijing Drumsong in the Liu Style." *Chinoperl Papers* 15: 69–83.

———. 2011. "A Peking Drumsong." In *The Columbia Anthology of Folk and Popular Literature*, edited by Victor H. Mair and Mark Bender, 406–412. New York: Columbia University Press.

Stickland, Leonie R. 2008. *Gender Gymnastics: Performing and Consuming Japan's Takarazuka Revue.* Melbourne: Trans Pacific Press.

Stock, Jonathan P.J. 2003. Huju: *Traditional Opera in Modern Shanghai*. Oxford: Oxford University Press.

Thompson, William Forde. 2009. *Music, Thought, and Feeling: Understanding the Psychology of Music.* New York: Oxford University Press.

Tsau, Shu-ying. 1979–80. *"Xiangsheng* and its Star Performer, Hou Baolin." *Chinoperl Papers* 9: 32–79.

Turner, Victor with Edie Turner. 2008. "Performing Ethnography." In *The Performance Studies Reader*, edited by Henry Bial, 2nd ed., 323–336. New York: Routledge.

Volpp, Sophie. 2011. *Worldly Stage: Theatricality in Seventeenth-Century China.* Cambridge, MA: Harvard University Asia Center.

Wallin, Nils L., Bjorn Merker, and Steven Brown, eds. 2000. *The Origins of Music.* Cambridge, MA: MIT Press.

Wang, David Der-wei. 2003. "Impersonating China." *Chinese Literature: Essays, Articles, Reviews* 25: 133–163.

Wang, Yuejin. 1991. "Red Sorghum: Mixing Memory and Desire." In *Perspectives on Chinese Cinema*, edited by Chris Berry, 80–103. London: BFI Publishing.

Wichmann, Elizabeth. 1991. *Listening to Theatre: The Aural Dimension of Beijing Opera.* Honolulu: University of Hawaii Press.

Williams, Sean and Lillis Ó Laoire. 2011. *Bright Star of the West: Joe Heaney, Irish Song Man.* Oxford: Oxford University Press.

Wolf, Margery. 1974. "Chinese Women: Old Skills in a New Context." In *Woman, Culture, and Society*, edited by Michelle Zimbalist Rosaldo and Louise Lamphere, 157–172. Stanford: Stanford University Press.

———. 1985 *Revolution Postponed: Women in Contemporary China*. Stanford: Stanford University Press.

Wu, Cuncun. 2004. *Homoerotic Sensibilities in Late Imperial China*. London: Routledge Curzon.

Wu, Yi-Li. 2010. *Reproducing Women: Medicine, Metaphor, and Childbirth in Late Imperial China.* Berkeley: University of California Press.

Yang, Mayfair Meihui. 1989. "The Gift Economy and State Power in China." *Comparative Studies in Society and History* 31 (1): 25–54.

———. 1994. *Gifts, Favors, and Banquets: The Art of Social Relationships in China.* Ithaca: Cornell University Press.

———. 1999. *Spaces of Their Own: Women's Public Sphere in Transnational China.* Minneapolis: University of Minnesota Press.

Yeh, Catherine. 2006. *Shanghai Love: Courtesans, Intellectuals, and Entertainment Culture, 1850–1910.* Seattle: University of Washington Press.

Zeitlin, Judith T. 2006. "'Notes of the Flesh' and the Courtesan's Song in Seventeenth-Century China." In *The Courtesan's Arts: Cross-Cultural Perspectives*, edited by Martha Feldman and Bonnie Gordon, 75–99. Oxford: Oxford University Press.

———. 2007. *The Phantom Heroine: Ghosts and Gender in Seventeenth-century Chinese Literature.* Honolulu: University of Hawaii Press.

———. 2014 *Performing Images: Opera in Chinese Visual Culture*. Chicago: Smart Museum of Art.

Zhang, Cuifeng. 1985. "The Autobiography of the Drum Singer, Jang Tsueyfenq (as told to Liou Fang)." Translated by Rulan Chao Pian. *Chinoperl Papers* 13 (1): 76–106.

Zhang, Souchen et al. 1983. *Traditional Comic Tales*. Translated by Gladys Yang. Beijing: Chinese Literature, distributed by China Publications.

Zhao, Mi. 2014. "From Singing Girl to Revolutionary Artist: Female Entertainers Remembering China's Socialist Past (1949-The Present)." *Twentieth Century China* 39 (2): 166–190.

Zhong, Xueping. 2000. *Masculinity Besieged: Issues of Modernity and Male Subjectivity in Chinese Literature of the Late Twentieth Century.* Durham, NC: Duke University Press.

Zieman, Katherine. 2008. *Singing the New Song: Literacy and Liturgy in Late Medieval England.* Philadelphia: University of Pennsylvania Press.

Index

(Figures are indexed in **bold** and Music Examples in italic)